D0518555

Bo‹
Fa
Fax

HAIG

MASTER OF THE FIELD

HAIG

MASTER OF THE FIELD

by

MAJOR-GENERAL SIR JOHN DAVIDSON
K.C.M.G., C.B., D.S.O.

Director of Operations in France
1916-1917-1918

Pen & Sword
MILITARY

First published in Great Britain in 1953 by Peter Nevill Ltd.

Reprinted in this format in 2010 by
Pen & Sword Military
An imprint of
Pen & Sword Books Ltd
47 Church Street
Barnsley
South Yorkshire
S70 2AS

ISBN 978 184884 362 2

Printed and bound in England
By CPI

Pen & Sword Books Ltd incorporates the Imprints of
Pen & Sword Aviation, Pen & Sword Family History, Pen & Sword Maritime,
Pen & Sword Military, Wharncliffe Local History, Pen & Sword Select,
Pen & Sword Military Classics, Leo Cooper, Remember When,
Seaforth Publishing and Frontline Publishing

For a complete list of Pen & Sword titles please contact
PEN & SWORD BOOKS LIMITED
47 Church Street, Barnsley, South Yorkshire, S70 2AS, England
E-mail: enquiries@pen-and-sword.co.uk
Website: www.pen-and-sword.co.uk

CONTENTS

Introduction by Marshal of the Royal Air Force
The Viscount Trenchard, GCB, OM, GCVO, DSO   vii

Foreword by the Author   xiii

Postscript to the Foreword   xxiii

Preface to the 2010 edition by Douglas Montagu-Douglas-Scott, OBE   xxv

Chapter

   I   EVENTS LEADING UP TO THE CRISIS IN 1917   1

   II   CONDITIONS OF THE ALLIED ARMIES—FRENCH, RUSSIAN AND ITALIAN—IN 1917   13

   III   OPERATIONS IN NORTHERN FLANDERS, PASSCHENDAELE,
FIRST PHASE—31ST JULY TO 31ST AUGUST   26

   IV   OPERATIONS IN NORTHERN FLANDERS, PASSCHENDAELE,
SECOND PHASE—1ST SEPTEMBER TO 7TH OCTOBER   41

   V   OPERATIONS IN NORTHERN FLANDERS, PASSCHENDAELE,
THIRD PHASE—7TH OCTOBER TO 13TH NOVEMBER   57

   VI   ORGANIZATION AND PREPARATION TO MEET GERMAN OFFENSIVE 1918   74

   VII   THE GERMAN OFFENSIVES OF 21ST MARCH AND 9TH APRIL 1918   84

   VIII   BRITISH OFFENSIVE 8TH AUGUST TO ARMISTICE 11TH NOVEMBER 1918   97

   IX   COMMENTS   109

   X   REVIEW   124

Appendix 1   An Article from *Blackwood's Magazine*, January 1944,
'The Bent Sword,' by A.M.G.   139

Appendix 2   The Preface to the *Official History France and Belgium,
Vol. II*, 1917, by kind permission of its author, Brigadier-
General Sir James Edmonds, CB, CMG, RE, Hon.D Litt
(Oxon), and with the authority of the Controller H.M.
Stationery Office.   148

Map 1   Passchendaele 1917   160

Map 2   Kaiserschlacht, 21st March, 1918   161

Map 3   Victory, 1918   162

INTRODUCTION

by *Marshal of the Royal Air Force*

THE VISCOUNT TRENCHARD, GCB, OM, GCVO, DSO

'It is only by studying the past
that we can foresee, however
dimly, or partially, the future.'

*Extract from speech by Mr Winston Churchill
at Guildhall 9th November 1951*

WHEN I was asked by my old friend, Sir John Davidson, the author of this book, to write the introduction, I was not only pleased and honoured but looked upon it as my duty to do so.

I know full well I cannot perform the task adequately, but I would like to say that everybody should read this book if they want to understand the situation in Britain and the British Commonwealth to-day.

I hope the views I express here may help the historians of the future to write accurately about Field-Marshal Earl Haig's influence on the world in those difficult days.

It has been the fashion, since 1918, to decry Haig's reputation as a man and as a soldier. This criticism is centred round the series of battles in France which took place over the years 1916, 1917 and 1918.

The power of this criticism, some of which has come from people in high positions, in my opinion has tended to dim the work of a great man and a great soldier.

Lord Haig took over the command of the British Armies in France in 1915.

The British Army of those days was a small one, compared with that of France, which was looked upon then as the greatest military power in the world. The French Army was supported by those of Italy and Russia, two other great powers, but they had to face the might of Germany and Austria, prepared and ready for total warfare.

I look upon the years 1916, 1917 and 1918 as a time of great change in the history of the British people. It was the turning point in the history of the world and of the British Empire.

During the years 1914-18 the following great changes took place:

1. In 1914 we were the leaders of the world, with our Dominions, Colonies and the great Indian Empire behind us. When the war ended we were still a great nation, but not the leaders of the world. The change in our status had begun.

2. The great prestige and tone of British public life was altered.

3. At the beginning of the war France had, or was thought to have, the most powerful army in the world. At the end of the war the French Army had lost that position and France was no longer a great military power.

4. When we entered the war the British fleet was immeasurably superior to any other; it had not been seriously challenged for over a hundred years. When the war ended that supremacy on the sea was threatened by the aeroplane and the submarine.

5. For the first time in the history of the British Empire we saw a British Army on the Continent comparable in size with the great continental armies.

6. Conscription was introduced in Britain for the first time.

7. For the first time in history a large British Army in the field was placed under a foreigner as Supreme Commander.

8. England was rationed for the first time.

9. Barbed wire was used for the first time in a large way in warfare. This resulted in an enormous increase in the number of guns and the amount of ammunition required to destroy the barbed wire.

10. The internal combustion engine was used for the first time in war.

11. It was the first time the aeroplane had been used in war. Although the air arm was small, it was seen and recognized that a new force had come into being; that England was no longer an island and that the Channel was merely an anti-tank ditch.

12. It was the first time tanks were used in war.

13. No single factor contributed more powerfully to the fundamental changes which characterized the era of the First World War than the development of wireless communication. The turn of the century had witnessed the genesis and early exploitation of this great scientific achievement; the impelling influence of war forced the growth of the new science, both in the fields of telegraphy and speech and in its widespread application to the requirements of land, sea and air warfare. Before hostilities ceased, progress had advanced to a stage of development which was destined in the years of peace to create such profound influence on the political, economic and social spheres of the world. Within a few years world-wide wireless communication systems were established and from 1924 onwards broadcasting gave simultaneous news to whole world communities on an ever-increasing scale.

14. Another change was the realization that some of the planets in the universe are millions and millions of miles away and space has no end. At the same time, space, and time, were contracting more drastically than at any other period of recorded history, due to wireless and the aeroplane.

It must be remembered that all these changes took place under the following conditions:

In 1916 the Army of France had been bled white and this affected the morale of the French nation.

In 1917 Russia was out of the war. Italy was on her knees and we were determined to fight on to victory, alone. I think in some ways we were more alone then than we were in 1940.

There were no flanks to be turned in France.

The loss of morale in France was followed by large-scale mutinous conduct within the French Armies, as is shown in the French official histories of the war, and in this book.

Haig recognized, as it was recognized in the Second World War by Mr. Churchill, Mr. Roosevelt and General Eisenhower, that it was essential that Germany had to be smashed in Europe and not elsewhere. As far as fighting was concerned, Haig had lost his allies, but he realized that Germany was the enemy, although many of the leading statesmen, generals, and others thought there was a short cut to victory, in the same way as people think they can stop a determined burglar by setting a booby trap in the lodge at the gates.

Haig knew, as few did, that it was touch and go whether France went out of the war. When morale begins to weaken, it may at any moment go with a rush—the smallest crack in the dam may produce an overwhelming flood.

He knew if France went out of the war the British Army on the Continent was doomed—four or five million men would have been lost. He knew if he fought on he would save not only Britain but the world.

In spite of the British Army having suffered heavy casualties during the battles of 1915, 1916 and 1917, the high standard of leadership of the young officers and non-commissioned officers showed no signs of deterioration.

In spite of all the differences of opinion about tactics, and the grumbling which inevitably goes on in any long war, the morale of the armies was excellent, due in a very large measure to the Commander-in-Chief. It never weakened. In fact at the Hindenburg Line in August 1918 it was greater than ever—there was no denying it. I feel if anyone but Haig had been in command then, and the break in the Hindenburg Line had not been accomplished, the war would have gone on quite easily for another year, if not two years.

Haig was inarticulate and this handicapped him greatly when talking to his officers or the men, in numbers or individually. He had no glib tongue, or the gift of words, but his spirit and morale were of the highest. The British Army's spirit of determination not to be beaten—to win in the end—was inspired by its Commander-in-Chief.

I am one of those who believed then, and still believe, that after the terrific battles of the Somme and Passchendaele, and the great offensive of April 1918, all ranks trusted Haig. Their faith in him was unshaken. This was shown particularly by the wonderful morale and spirit of the whole British Army on 8th August 1918, when, under Haig's leadership, the Army attacked with an enthusiasm that few at home realized, and the long-drawn-out struggle was ended. This was Haig's triumph.

I think the following illustrates this.

An officer of junior rank—a major—had taken his men, after they had fought for weeks and suffered appalling casualties, behind the line for a rest, but almost immediately they were ordered back to the front line again to fill another gap. The officer said he was sorry to have to haul them out and take them back. A sergeant turned round and said: 'Sir, we came to do a job—to defeat Germany, and we are going to do it.'

That was the spirit of Haig.

I feel one day in years to come—it may be fifty or even a hundred years—history will relate what the world owes to Haig, and this book I hope will help to show his difficulties and the strength of character he displayed in facing those difficulties and overcoming them.

TRENCHARD

December 1952

FOREWORD

by

MAJOR-GENERAL SIR JOHN DAVIDSON

KCMG, CB, DSO

Director of Military Operations at General Headquarters, 1916–17–18

I HAD felt some doubt as to the desirability of publishing these notes on the operations of 1917 and their aftermath of 1918, a period which has been the subject of so much controversy at home. There were three main reasons for hesitation.

Firstly, the French inevitably bore the main burden of the war from its outset to the conclusion of the Battle of Verdun in 1916, a fact which should not be lost sight of; thereafter the British then bore practically the whole burden from the Battle of the Somme in 1916, throughout the years 1917 and 1918, to its victorious conclusion. In other words we took two years to produce, equip and train an army of a continental calibre while the French were holding the enemy at bay. Thereafter the French Army, exhausted and dispirited by its prolonged effort, became incapable of further active operations of a major character and was compelled to stand by and witness the task taken over by us. Inevitably, therefore, I must be dealing with a period during which the British Army was in the ascendant both numerically and morally, while the French Army was sick at heart, suffering from a sense of disappointment and frustration, and, as General Gouraud termed it, 'entering the most critical period of the war, that bitter time of depression morale.' This presents rather an unenviable task.

Secondly, I must obviously probe this 'depression morale' and examine the degree of demoralization of the French Army which grew to a danger point during the prolonged, arduous and bloody defence of Verdun in 1916 and burst into open mutiny after the costly failure of Nivelle's grandiose operations in April 1917 on the Aisne. It is on the extent and intensity of this

xiii

demoralization, which developed over a wide area into open mutiny, that depended in large measure the attitude of the British Commander-in-Chief and the action of the British Army. The curtain of silence and secrecy which shrouded these mutinies was so effective, both at the time and long after, as to have created some sort of mystery. We now have the French Official History on this subject, as well as the *British Official History*—but somehow we still have some disbelievers who persist in saying that the French Mutiny was merely a figment of Haig's mind to excuse some of his military mistakes. This, of course, is the acme of stubborn stupidity or childish ignorance. But these croakers are gradually disappearing and truth will out eventually whatever the depth of the well may be.

Thirdly, it was Lord Haig's desire to avoid, either directly or indirectly, entering into any controversy connected with the conduct of the war. Others might and would naturally do so, but his wish was to leave judgement to the Official Historian (*Military Operations France and Belgium 1917*, Vol. II) who, he felt, after the passage of time, would be in a position to get the right perspective and to tell the truth. In this connection I would mention that on two occasions I wrote to Haig objecting to certain unjust and quite unwarranted criticisms levelled at him and suggested that I should take some action. On the first occasion he wrote to me in reply, dated 12th August 1919:—'I have no doubt that the Official History will do full justice to us all, so let us leave it at that.' On the second occasion Haig wrote on 4th March 1927—written a year before his death:—'Do as you think fit; personally I don't care what the papers say. I hope that the Official History will give the true story.' I have these two letters before me as I write.

I have waited for over thirty years for the publication of that volume of the Official History (referred to above) which deals with 1917, and I feel content with it—content in the sense that I feel Lord Haig would, in general, have been satisfied that it gives a reasonable account and a fair statement of fact.

Lord Trenchard, in his letter to *The Times* dated 26th January 1949, most appropriately drew attention to the publication of the volume and to its importance as a revelation of the truth. Impressed as I was with his letter, I felt that the truth might not reach the public generally as Official Histories have a very small and limited public. I therefore wrote to *The Times* on the 14th February recommending those who are interested in the 1917 phase of the war to read the eighteen pages of the Preface (written by the Official Historian) and the Retrospect of twenty-one pages, both of which will throw some light on hitherto obscure matters and will not occupy much time to peruse. I should like to take this opportunity of thanking both the Official Historian, Brigadier-General Sir James Edmonds, CB, CMG, and The Controller of H.M. Stationery Office, for their kind permission to quote from the volume as I wish, and to publish the Preface as a whole in full, which I have done as an appendix to this book.

Since the issue of the Official History, I have received a number of letters requesting that I should publish such records or notes that I may have on the subject of the war in 1917 and 1918. I quote a typical letter from one who had commanded a Corps in Flanders during the period under review. He wrote a letter to me dated 18th February 1949:—'My reason for writing to you is that you are perhaps one of the few remaining Officers who were on Haig's Staff who knows the whole truth about that period of the fighting. Would it not be wise therefore to let the facts be known rather more widely than by your letter to *The Times* (14th February 1949) or Edmonds' Preface. I think for Haig's reputation something should be done.'

Feeling that Lord Haig would have been generally satisfied with the Official History, I concluded at first that no comments from me were either necessary or desirable. On second thoughts I felt that I was free and in a position to throw some light on certain aspects of the campaigns, and, in doing so, I would have had the approval not only of the Commander-in-Chief but also of the Commanders of the 2nd, 3rd and 4th Armies, all of whom, after a speech which I made in the House of Commons* on 6th August 1919 and in which I reviewed the events of 1917 and 1918, expressed to me their concurrence with what I had said. Lord Haig wrote to me on the 12th:—'I was very pleased to see

* See Hansard.

from Hansard how well you spoke out in the House regarding the critical period we went through in 1917. For this I thank you and congratulate you.' This speech was summarized in the notes to pages 127 and 128 in *Sir Douglas Haig's Despatches*.

General The Honble. Sir Herbert Lawrence, who had served in the 17th Lancers and in the South African War with Lord Haig, and who was his Chief of Staff throughout 1918, had consistently advised and urged me to place on record such information as I possessed. He regarded it of importance and, on his death, he left me his papers connected with that period. General Sir Douglas Baird, who was for a long period on Lord Haig's Staff both in India and France and who subsequently commanded an Army in India, as well as Lt.-General Sir Bertie Fisher, who was in the 17th Lancers with Lord Haig and was subsequently Colonel of that Regiment—both close friends of his—expressed their views to me that some such record as I now propose should be published.

To Dr C. E. W. Bean, the Australian Official Historian, I owe my special thanks for his ready consent that I should quote from *The Official History of Australia in the War of 1914–18*, which deals in such detail and so graphically with the middle or second phase of the Passchendaele operations (the actions of 20th and 26th September and 4th October) in 1917, which had so important a bearing on bringing the war to a successful conclusion in 1918, a year earlier than was expected by experts in all allied countries, including our own. Lord Haig was the exception, for he had persistently predicted that 1918 would witness the defeat of the German Army.

The six months May to November 1917 in fact registered a definite turn of the tide, and the extraordinary feature about it is that it was during this particular period that all our operating Allies collapsed, the French in mutiny, the Russians in revolution, and the Italians in defeat, leaving us to face the enemy alone. It must also be remembered that it was during this time that the First Sea Lord stated to the War Cabinet that: 'If the Army cannot get the Belgian Ports, the Navy cannot hold the Channel and the war is as good as lost. . . . It is no good making plans for next year.'* A still more extraordinary feature is that it was the conduct of the war during this period that was more severely criticized than any other. What a succession of unprecedented calamities!

Here is a record of such dangers and anxieties which beset the British Commander-in-Chief that I can think of no parallel in history. Yet the tide had begun to turn without any shadow of doubt; all evidence regarding the decline in morale of the German Army and people clearly proves the truth of that assertion. The flow of the tide became stronger and deeper and the moral decline of Germany was accentuated as America's declaration of war became known and the time of arrival of their Army approached.

It has been my object in this book to examine this turn of the tide in the autumn of 1917 (Chapters III, IV, and V) and its corollary in 1918 (Chapters VI, VII and VIII), for in 1918 events followed in natural sequence.

I feel, however, that I am justified in referring to a much more important movement, a revolutionary movement, a wider and deeper tide, indeed nothing short of a turn in history which had been developing for some little time and which experienced a sudden and explosive impetus by the outbreak of war in 1914. Almost instantaneously there was a break in the old order of things and the seeds of a new order which had been lying dormant came to life in nearly every country in the world. Moreover the world was beginning to shrink rapidly in space and time, bringing the nations into closer contact with each other. Great Britain was no longer insulated from major wars. Physical science had advanced with rapid strides, especially the science of destruction, while human nature and humane feeling had made little progress, if any. Political changes and tendencies, and the clash of ideologies were becoming accentuated. Old ideas had to be discarded or revised and new ideas assimilated and adjusted to meet new conditions. Every field of activity was being affected by the turn and turmoil of the changed and changing outlook, throwing up problems of great complexity whose solution and adaptation were urgent.

* See Official History.

At the outbreak of the First World War we had no previous experience of the application of compulsory military service. The production of a National Army presented many new problems. The rapid expansion of our Defence Forces with their technical and auxiliary services; their organization and administration; the supply of arms and equipment keeping pace with the latest developments; the vast increase in munitions; the adjustment of labour in relation to demands for personnel of the fighting services with the requirements of manpower for production of all descriptions, warlike and other; the demands for increased transport facilities both on land and at sea.

These were only some of the matters to be resolved in the establishment of a nation in arms, but there were others equally important, affecting an army in the field of a continental calibre operating on foreign soil; such, for example, as control and command, co-ordination of effort, the relationship of the Government with the Military Commands, Army, Navy and Air Force; the relationship of the Allies with each other on all matters civil and military connected with the war; Unity of Command and the responsibility for the safety of the Army. I shall deal with some of these subjects in Chapters VI, VII and VIII and in my comments in Chapter IX.

A subject of the first importance was the development of the internal combustion engine as applied to warfare. Except as a means of rapid transport this was still in its infancy on the outbreak of the First World War. The whole subject of its use from invention to production was speeded up, more especially in relation to aircraft and tanks. In spite of the obvious value and the efficient handling of both these modern weapons, they had only a relatively minor effect on the operations in the early days of the war. This was inevitably due to their scarcity and performance. Rapid progress was, however, being made all through the war both in design and production. The development of the Royal Flying Corps during the war was remarkable; the demand for its services and the variety of its many duties became so insistent that the Government instituted an enquiry into the organization of the Corps especially in the direction of bombing and fighting, reconnaissance and co-operation with the ground forces, etc. This resulted in the establishment in April 1918 of an Air Ministry and the formation of the Royal Air Force with Major-General Sir Hugh Trenchard as the first Chief of the Air Staff. One cannot help wondering what would have happened in the First World War if we had had the immense power and superiority in the air which was developed in the Second World War. There seemed to be no limit in the continued progress of power and speed in the air.

Amongst many other difficulties were the repudiation of our debt to America which had accumulated during the war and an adverse trade balance which began to be an anxiety—both of these symptoms of much greater difficulties which would arise with debts accumulated and accumulating if we came to be involved in another war. But I must not deal with post-war finance and economics as they hardly come within the scope of this book.

The feature of the 1914–18 War is that after October 1914 until March 1918 the war was static from the Belgian coast to Switzerland. There was no vulnerable flank to turn. The front was fortified with a series of trenches protected by wire and automatic and quick-firing weapons with great fire power, and with mobile reserves which could be quickly moved to any threatened point. This was a species of siege warfare which had not even the mobility or power of manœuvre of the old-fashioned wars of fortresses. It was largely a matter of the power of destruction to effect a breach in the defences; the only alternative was the type of warfare indulged in at the opening of the 1939 war —a passive and what might almost be known as a 'cold' war, which might continue at vast expense with no casualties, no decision and no end. In World War I the result of any attack became after some experience a matter of mathematics. One could reasonably expect, and usually achieved, the result that the breach or depth of penetration into the enemy's fortifications would amount to about half the length of the base of attack. Unless the base could be widened *pari passu* with the depth of penetration, which was never the case, the attack would gradually fade away and be brought to a halt. Moreover, the casualties in offence and defence were usually about equal.

This happened over and over again, until, in the autumn of 1917 in what I call the second phase of the battle for Passchendaele, siege operations were adopted at the three battles on 20th September (Menin Road), 26th September (Polygon Wood) and 4th October (Broodseinde) when the Australians smashed up the defences and destroyed the German counter-stroke divisions as they appeared, by attacking at intervals of four or five days to a depth of only from 1,200 to 1,500 yards under an overwhelming artillery barrage 1,000 yards deep. On the last day, 4th October, the Australian Official History says:— 'An overwhelming blow had been struck and both sides knew it.' . . . and 'No army could continue to withstand such blows' —but more of this in its proper place.

In all this welter of changes, new conditions, mutinies, rebellions, defeats and every kind of difficulty, Lord Haig was a pattern of imperturbability and concentration on his main object—victory. German military opinion describes him thus:— 'The circumstances that Haig could not act really independently but always had to make his decisions subject to conditions imposed on him, is no reason to deny him the position of a Commander-in-Chief. Dependence on others was often the fate of great Commanders. What is more important is whether his actions were conducted with strategic ability, firm will, strength of character, acceptance of responsibility and political insight. Haig possessed all these qualities and used them in harmonious combination, as Clausewitz requires of a great Commander. By means of these powers, he saved France in 1916 and 1917 and pre-eminently on that historic day, 26th March 1918. Finally.... He really remained "MASTER OF THE FIELD".'

I cannot help referring to his determination, moral courage, military knowledge, foresight and long sight and even second sight, his unswerving loyalty and imperturbability throughout adversity and good fortune alike, his equable relations with his Allies who were failing him but were, at the same time, receiving his unfailing help and sympathy throughout their difficulties. But perhaps even more I would refer to his attitude to intrigue; to have him replaced; to place him and his great Army of the Empire and Commonwealth under an untried

French commander who was committed to a hazardous enter-
prise at a time when the French Army was known to be at a
very low ebb; and finally to have the opinion of French generals
canvassed as to his capacity for command. I would mention
here a quotation from W. B. Maxwell in *Time Gathered*, p. 243:—
'We believed firmly in Haig; we trusted him absolutely; we
followed him blindly.' He gave the remainder of his life after
the war to the welfare of the men who had fought under his
command.

This book does not attempt to give any running account of
the operations in France and Flanders during 1917 and 1918.
My object has been only to give such a historical and continuous
outline as I thought necessary, in order to deal with certain
crises and episodes, and to analyse important decisions reached,
as well as to examine the results of those decisions in their proper
place and order. I know the truth about most of the controversial
subjects, having not only been at the relative conferences and
discussions, but also having been in the Field-Marshal's confidence, and heard his views on all manners of matters and
subjects when he was in the mood to talk or think aloud; but
this was on rare occasions, for often on long motor or other
journeys he was silent.

There are so many doubting Thomases that I have on every
possible occasion quoted at great length from official accounts
and from other reliable sources; from the French about their
own troubles, from the Germans about British criticisms of
their own British military achievements, from the Australians
about their own successful battles in September and October
1917 on the Passchendaele Ridge, and again from the Germans
about their own failures. Indeed, I fear I have filled this book
with quotations and I have done so advisedly, for they carry
weight and support to my arguments. I offer no apologies either
for these or for the many repetitions which I have used for
purposes of emphasis.

Apart from those to whom I have already referred, I desire
to tender my thanks to the Viscount Norwich, PC, GCMG, DSO,
for giving me permission to quote from *Haig*, Vol. II. To Major-
General Sir Edward Spears, KBE, CB, MC, for allowing me to

quote from *Prelude to Victory*, and I would like in this connection to draw attention to his interesting account in that book of the Calais Conference held on 26th February 1917, at which the Commander-in-Chief and the British Army were placed under the command of a French general who, within three months, was deposed; also, to Sir Philip Gibbs for permitting me to quote from his book *From Bapaume to Passchendaele*.

I wish to offer my thanks to the Librarian of the Imperial War Museum for his ready help; to the New Zealand Authorities for permission to quote from their official War History; and once again to Brigadier-General Sir James Edmonds for his leave to make similar references to his *Short History of World War I*.

Lastly, I offer my deep thanks to Marshal of the Royal Air Force Viscount Trenchard, GCB, OM, GCVO, DSO, for his encouragement, and for consenting to write the Introduction to this book.   J. H. D.

Postscript to Foreword

Just before closing this book I received a copy of the *Private Papers of Douglas Haig, 1914–1919*, edited by Robert Blake. It was the first time I had read or seen any part of Haig's Diaries.

So far as the controversy on personalities is concerned, my feeling is exactly described by the *Yorkshire Post*, in which is expressed the view that Haig's strong self-contained character found the relief it needed in the private expression of feelings which were repressed in public or in conversation. I am however chiefly concerned with Robert Blake's interesting Introduction and comments which lend themselves to some debate.

Shortly after the publication of the Diaries, there followed a review by Arthur Bryant in the *Illustrated London News* of 6th December 1952 in which his opening remarks drew the attention of the nation—and none too soon—to an event which has been half forgotten and half ignored, namely, 'The total and irretrievable defeat between 8th August and 11th November 1918 of the German Imperial Army—the greatest war machine the world has ever seen—by a British Army.'

Both these publications, the Diaries and the review, have been most valuable in emphasizing the great and unique services rendered by Lord Haig to his country, and will help to guide public opinion in the right direction in the future.

It has been my endeavour in this book to work to the same end, but from a different angle. From my close association with the Field-Marshal during the period under review, and from my knowledge of the crises and problems as they arose, I have felt it incumbent on me to expose certain inaccuracies and misconceptions which have in large measure arisen out of the secrecy and mystery surrounding the French mutinies, and have gained credence owing to the long delay in publication of the relative volumes of the Official Histories.

For example, the Commander-in-Chief has been suspected of giving misleading information to the Prime Minister and War Cabinet regarding the condition of the French Army and Pétain's ability to co-operate actively with the British. The transmission of information in this connection to the War Cabinet was not the duty of Haig; it was the duty of the Chief of the Imperial General Staff, Field-Marshal Sir William Robertson, who reported fully on such matters, and especially on the 20th June 1917, an important date, just one month before the Flanders offensive was launched.

It probably has never been realized, or never been known, that this offensive directly caused the abandonment of a German offensive of thirty divisions in the summer of 1917 projected by German Imperial Headquarters to probe the French defences in the direction of Paris. Thus the French Army was effectively saved when the French mutinies were at their height. (British Official History. German Official History.)

The time seems to have arrived with the publication of the Official Histories of Great Britain, Australia, New Zealand, Germany and France, followed by the Diaries of the British Commander-in-Chief, that, in the final words of Arthur Bryant's review, 'we can begin to see what a British Army accomplished'; and, if I may add, why the Germans have rated Haig, on the conclusion of hostilities, as remaining 'Master of the Field'.

J. H. D.

PREFACE TO THE 2010 EDITION
by Douglas Montagu-Douglas-Scott, OBE

Major-General Sir John Davidson DSO, KCMG, CB, the author of this important book, was Director of Military Operations for my grandfather, Field Marshal Earl Haig, from 1915 until the end of the First World War. He was thus in a key position to understand and write authoritatively about the battles of the Somme (the first time France was saved by the British), Third Ypres, often known as Passchendaele (the second time France was rescued from almost certain defeat), the crushing of the German attacks in 1918, known as the Kaiserschlacht, and the British victories from 8 August 1918 until Armistice.

'Tavish' Davidson was born in July 1876 and was commissioned from Sandhurst into the 60th Rifles in 1896. He saw service in South Africa, before going to the Staff College in 1905. Thereafter he had a number of appointments as a staff officer, including two years at the War Office, during the vital period, 1908-10, when Haldane and Haig laid the foundations for the Territorial Army and planned the expeditionary force, which went to France in 1914. After the war he became the Member of Parliament for Fareham until retiring in 1931 to look after his business interests. He died in December 1954 only a year after the first publication of *Haig: Master of the Field*.

It is a great pleasure to have been asked to write the Preface for this new Edition of Tavish Davidson's book covering the dramatic events of 1917 and 1918. The first edition, published by Peter Nevill in 1953, seems to have had rather a limited influence on military historians. Too many writers, anxious to sell books about this crucial period of the First World War, have sought to denigrate the outstanding professionalism of Douglas Haig, his team of Army Commanders and the staff officers who served them by use of selective quotations, twisting facts and straightforward invention.

Did any German General in the First World War really refer to the British Army as 'Lions led by Donkeys'? No, the nearest we can get to this is that the Russian General may have said it in the Crimean War. Did senior staff officers really not know the condition of the ground in the early and final stages of Third Ypres? Of course they did and they also knew that conditions were even worse for the Germans, because the natural drainage of rain-water from the Passchendaele-Roulers Ridge was away from Ypres and through the German defensive lines. The C-in-C also knew that the French Armies were not in any condition to defend themselves because of the mutinies, that the Russians were about to leave the war and that the Italians were groggy in the extreme. He was also aware of the tremendous loss of merchant ships from German submarines and thus the strategically vital objective of capturing the Channel ports, where the U-boats were based. Were the British casualties really more than 400,000 in Third Ypres? No, the official figure is 238,000, bad enough certainly but the campaign kept the French in the war and laid the foundations for the defeat of the *Kaiserschlacht* in the first part of 1918 and 'the 100 Days' of victory in the second half.

'Historians' hoping to find support for their pet sensational theory will not find it in Tavish's book. The book is a straightforward, factual account of what happened and why, by a senior staff officer who was there and closely involved in the planning and execution of battles. The Third Ypres battles are dealt with at length, covering almost half the book with the *Kaiserschlacht* and 'the 100 Days' together forming most of the second half of the book. The final chapters deal with the effect of poor French morale. Attached to the book are two Appendixes. The first is an article from *Blackwood's Magazine* dated January 1944 and written by someone with the initials A.M.G. It deals in detail with the French mutinies. The second article is an extract from the *British Official History* covering the period June to November 1917. The extract quotes from an article in the *News Chronicle* of 25 March 1935;

> 'Why has not Haig been recognised as one of England's greatest generals? Why, as a national figure, did he count far less than Lord Roberts, whose wars were picnics by comparison? The answer may be given in one word – "Passchendaele".

'Davidson makes an unanswerable case for the Third Ypres Campaign. He explains the strategic background of the failure of Britain's allies Russia and Italy, the need to capture ports from which the German submarine fleet operated and the crisis resulting from the French Army mutinies. He describes the battle of Broodseinde, including Menin Road and Polygon Wood. The German High Command considered the final phase of the battle as 'The Black Day of October 4th' yet, when Britain commemorated Passchendaele in 2007, there was little if any mention of Broodseinde in the media. All we were told about was that the first phase of the campaign in August was dreadful and that very little ground was captured.

General Davidson was well aware that his book would not be a popular book in the sense of high volume sales. In a letter, dated 4 September 1952, to my mother (Victoria, second daughter of Earl Haig) to whom he had sent a pre-production copy of the book, he wrote;

> '.......I much appreciate all you say & am deeply grateful to you. I agree with you that the book will not have a wide public & as you rightly say it will be limited to students of history, to military establishments etc., but what I think is important is that it will be treated as a book of reference & help to correct some historical errors and false conceptions.

> I have tried to show up your father's wonderful qualities under the most abnormal conditions and in critical situations. He will grow in stature as the years go by.......'

Sadly the book did little 'to correct some historical errors and false conceptions'. Most of the 'historians' evidently preferred their errors and misconceptions. They usually list *Haig: Master of the Field* in their bibliography, but there was little evidence that they actually read what General Davidson said about the unfolding drama of 1917 and 1918.

Tavish's judgement that my grandfather 'will grow in stature as the years go by' has started to come true. Let us hope that this edition of his fine book will help the process.

Bemersyde
April 2010

Editor's Note: Sadly Douglas Montagu-Douglas-Scott died prior the publication of this Edition. He edited Douglas Haig's Diaries and Letters 1861-1914: The Preparatory Prologue *(Pen and Sword Military, 2006).*

CHAPTER I

Events leading up to the French Crisis
April–May 1917

No doubt the French Revolution and the Napoleonic Wars affected the character and mentality of the French nation; the former in relation to its political stability, while the latter bled the manhood of the country white. Such dynamic events could not leave a nation untouched.

Just over half a century from the termination of the Napoleonic Wars, the Franco-Prussian War broke out, with its disastrous result to France, known to all, in which inefficiency, inadequate equipment, unreadiness and miscalculation played their part. The collapse was rapid, for the war was virtually over in a matter of a few months.

Just under half a century then elapsed before the outbreak of World War I during which time there was political stress and change, the development of class-consciousness and industrialisation. These latter provided some breeding-ground for unrest, pacifism and the spread of subversive propaganda. Some turbulent individuals and mischievous organizations rose to the surface as the new century opened, and these came home to roost soon after the outbreak of war in 1914.

Nevertheless, when this first world war broke out, the general mobilization of the French Army of some sixty-five divisions was carried out with efficiency and without any trouble. The reservists flocked to the colours punctually; indeed with patriotic fervour, and with an insignificant number of deserters. The trouble-makers were not even taken into custody as a precautionary measure. Patriotic songs and martial music were the order of the day. The offensive spirit was being encouraged by the military chiefs, who discarded the policy of fighting behind defensive works and within the fortress areas. Indeed many of the unsettling influences of the past years were swept away and submerged in a wave of patriotism.

This splendid spirit was somewhat damped by the retreat which featured the first phase of the war and was caused by the German outflanking movement through Belgium, but the spirit was in part restored by the advance from the River Marne to the River Aisne which saved Paris and checked the enemy's further progress.

Thereafter the opposing armies gradually settled down, locked in a close and deadly grip from the Belgian coast to Switzerland, which seemed to offer no quick solution and presaged a long war of exhaustion and attrition, no flank to turn, no overwhelming Air Force and no armoured superiority. It was from this moment that the strain on the fighting soldier began to tell as time passed, in degree as his exhaustion, war weariness, constant and heavy toll of casualties and hopeless outlook worked on his nervous system and reacted to the defeatist propaganda to which he was being increasingly subjected.

As the year 1915 came to a close Haig was appointed Commander-in-Chief of the British Forces in France and Belgium and witnessed almost at once the growing strain on the French Army and concurrently the growing strength and power of the British Army. He undoubtedly envisaged and foresaw the increasingly difficult and responsible task ahead when it ultimately and inevitably would become his duty to take the lead.

This earlier period of the war which may be reckoned as lasting from late 1914 to after the Verdun operations in 1916 is an important period and requires examination. It constitutes a period of two years of solid hardship and exposure to which the French Army was more generally and particularly exposed. Death or wounds appeared to be about the only alternatives. This was not unnaturally biting into the vitals of the average *poilu*, who was by nature highly strung and temperamental.

This atmosphere and these conditions were accentuated during the bloody fighting of Verdun in 1916. Pétain, who had assumed command in this area, 'watched an endless line of men marched up the Sacred Way to the Verdun battlegrounds and submitted themselves to a casualty list of between three and four hundred thousand. Seventy-eight French divisions passed up this Sacred Way and through the grinding mill of sacrifice.'

Meanwhile the British Battle of the Somme was launched on the 1st July and immediately had the effect of easing the situation at Verdun to the relief of the French. The Germans had been halted and the French had even recaptured the forts of Vaux and Douaumont in offensive actions respectively commanded by Mangin and Nivelle. This was the crucial moment when the British began to take the strain to an important and increasing degree in relief of the French and to draw the German attention to themselves.

But already the conditions had begun to affect the morale of the French Army, and it was evident from secret reports that the French soldier was being seriously tried and that the strain on him was ever growing. There were two methods employed by the French authorities to test the spirit and ascertain the feelings—in other words the morale—of the soldier and the trend of his mind. There was the Secret Service, with its observers specially selected, who were allocated to formations to mix with the troops and report the conversational tone; and there was also the Postal Control or Censorship whose duty it was to study the post-bags and report the written word. Each of these sources of information corroborated the tale of the other. By the end of 1916 there developed increasingly and seriously a tale of discouragement and exhaustion, of too long occupation of the trenches, too short a period of leave, ignorance of the object of their action, inadequate pay, medical and hospital arrangements, bad conditions of billets and indifferent food, no welfare organization, and no future to look forward to. To this was added a constant and growing stream of subversive propaganda; defeatist and pacifist leaflets distributed widely both in the front and in the rear of the armies as well as in many large cities. Over and above all this was the general question— What are the British doing and why don't they pull their weight?

3

I had heard a good deal of all this at the time from a source which I regarded and still regard as quite reliable and I am satisfied that the reports of both the Observer and Postal controls did at the time reach the Heads of both the French civil and military authorities. (The gist of these reports were subsequently circulated confidentially.)

It must have been fairly clear to Haig at two meetings which took place in May 1916, the first with Joffre on the 26th of that month and the second with President Poincaré on the 31st, that both displayed great anxiety regarding the German offensive at Verdun which was in its fourth month.

At the first of these meetings which took place at G.H.Q. Marshal Joffre pressed vehemently for the British attack on the Somme to be launched earlier to ease the French situation, which was evidently giving him cause for serious worry, and he pointed out the heavy losses and strain to which the French Army was being subjected. When Haig hesitated about advancing the date, Joffre lost his temper and expostulated in a loud voice that 'The French Army would cease to exist if we did nothing till August.'* A compromise was ultimately arranged, satisfactory to both, and calm restored. The date was fixed for the 1st July.

The second meeting was only five days later at Dury. Here Poincaré was accompanied by his Prime Minister and War Minister, also Joffre and Foch. Poincaré had just been to Verdun, where he had seen Pétain and Nivelle. It was the same story, that Verdun would fall if we did not attack soon; it was the same anxiety over the strain being imposed on the French Army, and their diminished reserves. Haig confirmed the date 1st July for the opening of the Somme battle, which Joffre had accepted, but in view of further overtures by Poincaré he promised to put forward the date to 25th June (but later at the request of the French it was put back again to 1st July). Meanwhile General des Vallières, a most reliable officer, liaison officer at G.H.Q., reported, 'Situation at Verdun serious. Not only men but Generals and staff are getting tired and jumpy.'

---

* I have vivid recollections of this interview at which I was present.

The responsible persons in the French Government and Army were obviously well aware of the serious strain on the French troops and that they were giving evidence of this strain.

I quote here from a secret report drawn up at G.H.Q. at the time and both approved and annotated by Haig:

> The British Commander-in-Chief had to estimate how much could be expected from our allies—especially the French—and to gauge the morale of their troops, the material means at their disposal, and the feelings of the High Command, the Government, and the country—on his judgement of this he had to decide on the rôle for the British Army which would be likely to give the best results for the general cause of the Allies.
>
> The evidence available was not altogether reassuring as to what the French would and could undertake in 1916. They evidently felt, and many openly said that it was time their British allies took a heavier share of the burden. The temper of the Army itself was not quite certain. It was therefore in doubt how much the French Army could and would undertake, how much the French Government would let it undertake, and with how much constancy and energy an offensive could be maintained by it in the face of great difficulty and heavy losses. . . . The severity of the Verdun fighting had very evidently left its mark on the French Army and on G.Q.G. Things were very critical with the French towards the end of the Verdun battle, and there had been unmistakable symptoms of demoralization, always particularly dangerous with French troops. It was no doubt in consequence of this that so much anxiety was shown at the Chantilly Conference in November 1916 to forestall any German attack in the spring of 1917.

As I have stated, the Somme battle began on 1st July and it continued intermittently until early November. It immediately took the strain off the French Army. It was subsequently admitted by Ludendorf that the Germans had sustained heavy losses, first at Verdun then at the Somme, almost continuously for nearly nine months and were at a very low ebb.

The active operations for 1916 were virtually at an end, and a conference was called by Joffre for 15th November at Chantilly to discuss the campaign for the following year, 1917.

This important conference at Chantilly, over which Joffre presided, came to the following conclusions:

1. That there should be a concentration of effort in the main theatre of operations, namely France.

2. That there should be a combined Franco-British offensive prepared to take place early in the year, co-ordinated with the offensives to be undertaken by the other allies.
3. That the main effort in this Franco-British offensive should be undertaken by the British.
4. That the British should mount an offensive later in the year in the North (for clearance of the Belgian coast).

Joffre, Haig and Robertson were all present at this meeting and there was general agreement. Joffre had warned his Government that to place undue strain on the French Army would be to court danger. It had been exhausted by the long-drawn-out struggle at Verdun. The British generals did not require to be told this, they knew it, but the French Cabinet did not receive the advice well (indeed it was the undoing of Joffre, as will be seen later).

Before the end of December Joffre was retired and created a Marshal of France. He actually put forward as his successor the name of Nivelle, who had commanded an army at Verdun, and had achieved a reputation of drive as well as care and precision of preparation, as a result of his recapture of the fort of Douaumont. But he was quite untried for the high command.

A meeting took place on the 20th December 1916 at Cassel between Haig and Nivelle at which the latter's project for the 1917 offensive was explained. This project aimed at the destruction of the principal mass of the enemy armies on the Western Front and involved:

(a) a main attack by three French armies on the Aisne front,
(b) a subsidiary attack by the British Army on the Arras front to precede the main attack and draw away the enemy reserves,
(c) vigorous exploitation.

This was a complete *bouleversement* of the Chantilly plan which had been agreed by Haig and Joffre, and which had been based on deliberate wearing-down action and on the assumption that the French Army was exhausted. It is almost inconceivable that such a change of view and of plan should have been substituted within a few weeks. Haig, though sceptical of the power of the French Army to carry out the part allotted to it in so ambitious a programme, lent his support to Nivelle in so far as the action of the British Army was concerned, and agreed to recast the operation plan already worked out for the coming spring.

Many points of difference between the two commanders arose, such as the taking over more of the front line from the French to release the latter's troops for active operations, the question of the date of attack and the timing of the offensives of all the Allies, the question of transportation facilities and the capacity of the Nord Railway, and so on. All these matters and others were referred by Nivelle to his Government and through it to London; with the result that a Cabinet meeting was held in London on the 15th January, both Haig and Nivelle being present, and the following conclusions reached:

(*a*) Relief of French front line to Amiens-Roye road,
(*b*) Offensive to start 1st April at latest,
(*c*) Plan as already agreed,
(*d*) If success expected is not gained, the battle to stop by agreement to allow British operations in the North to clear the Belgian coast.

The work of preparation for the offensive went ahead, but much hampered by the lack of transportation facilities which were almost entirely absorbed by the French, and lack of opportunity for training owing to requirements of men for railway construction and other work.

Meanwhile, when Joffre was removed from the Chief Command to make room for Nivelle, he was provided with an office in the École de Guerre in Paris where he could receive visitors and where he could be consulted. As I had known him and seen him fairly frequently during the past year, I took the opportunity of visiting him on one or two occasions in his new office when he appeared to be pleased to meet British officers and he talked quite frankly to me. On every occasion he took the opportunity of repeating to me that the French Army was *epuisée* and that we must not expect too much of it. He was quite clearly anxious about the rôle which it was now assuming, i.e. an offensive *à outrance*. He had expressed the view to his Government while he was still Commander-in-Chief that his armies required nursing during 1917 and that no considerable effort should be expected of them. He impressed me with his sincerity. I reported these conversations to the Chief of Staff, and to Haig.

A little earlier in the winter a mission was being despatched to Russia under Lord Milner, regarding, among other matters, the dispatch of British war material, including heavy artillery, to the Russian Army. Haig instructed me to accompany the mission as I was acquainted generally with the position of our war material in France, and particularly our requirements in heavy artillery, and I knew Haig's views on the dissipation of our strength. I left France and was on the point of leaving London with the mission when I received a telegram from Headquarters instructing me to return to France at once. I was glad to return, having a feeling that trouble was brewing, as indeed was the case.

A plot was hatched between Paris and London for placing the whole of the operations on the Western Front under the French Commander-in-Chief. This plot was known as 'The Calais Conference,' which took place on 26th and 27th February 1917 and at which both Prime Ministers Briand and Lloyd George, as well as the four Generals Lyautey, Nivelle, Robertson and Haig were present.

At the British Prime Minister's request the French produced a detailed scheme of organization for an Allied G.H.Q. in France. This provided for a French Generalissimo, and Headquarters Staff composed of French and British officers with a British Chief of Staff. The British Commander-in-Chief was to be retained, but only in name, and his duties were limited to those appertaining to the Adjutant-General's branch; he was to have nothing to do with operations.

Lyautey and Nivelle both disclaimed having seen the document until they were in the train on the way to Calais. Robertson was in complete ignorance of its existence, and no intimation whatever had been received by Haig that such a subject was to be brought up at this conference which had been convened ostensibly to deal with the very serious transport and railway difficulties.

It is not necessary for me to enter into the details of intrigue, discussions, the talks in confidence in different rooms, and some radical alterations and adjustments, which eventually produced a *modus operandi* to which Haig agreed—reluctantly—but with the will to make it work to the best of his ability. There were other problems unresolved, such for example as the German withdrawal and whether they were withdrawing to the Hindenburg Line in order to set free more reserves for the forthcoming battles, and whether or not the Vimy Ridge should be included in the British attack, and the very fortunate determination of Haig to include it in spite of much remonstrance and advice from Nivelle. The British Prime Minister was of course aware of this surprise which was to be sprung on the soldiers, indeed he was responsible for it.

This interesting but unpleasant episode of the Calais Conference is admirably told by General Sir Edward Spears in his book *Prelude to Victory*. It shows up well Haig's difficulties and the subtle efforts to undermine his authority at a very critical moment.

I must here refer to a visit paid by General Sir Noel Birch, chief artillery adviser, and myself to the area of the French offensive on the Aisne, a week or so before the British assault was launched. This visit was ostensibly made in view of the disagreement as to transport and railway facilities available to the respective armies, but we were also anxious to see how the French preparations were progressing, and ascertain the general atmosphere. We were amazed at the vast number of trains head to tail, blocked for want of unloading facilities, the level crossings being closed in most instances for long periods, thereby blocking the road transport movement. There appeared to be something wrong with the control and there was obviously much more rolling stock and many more road vehicles than could be handled properly. We had a talk with General Mangin, who criticized Haig's determination to attack Vimy—he was very sceptical about it—and we moved from Army Headquarters through corps, divisions and brigades to see the forward positions and were struck by the optimism and satisfaction at the rear, and as we went forward such feelings evaporated and a less confident tone was observed. On our return the Chief of Staff instructed us to report personally to Haig, which we did.

c

When reporting to Haig I invariably told him the unvarnished truth so far as I saw it, and so I did on this occasion; he listened to me with attention as usual, but warned me that all of us, himself included, must be most correct in our attitude to our allies and we must be careful always to say nothing carelessly which might in any way damage confidence in them—a most correct attitude which he invariably adopted. But it is ridiculous and utterly wrong to suppose that we did not invariably report everything, good, bad or indifferent, on every occasion, and he invariably listened with the greatest attention and with much cross-examination. He always expected his staff to be quite frank with him.

The great offensive was almost due to be launched and in what an impossible position did the British Commander-in-Chief find himself. The British Army had been placed under a French General who was quite untried, and who was engaged to undertake an all-out offensive to break the German Army and drive it back over the frontier with his armies, concerning whose steadfastness and morale there was considerable and grave doubt; there was great anxiety regarding the English Channel on account of the submarine menace, forcibly presented by the Admiralty, and the necessity for freeing the Belgian coast including Ostend and Zeebrugge; there was the Russian (Kerensky) revolution in progress and gradually developing into a more acute Bolshevist Revolution and thence without doubt into complete dissolution, with a consequent release of many German divisions in prospect from the Eastern to the Western Front; the Italians constituted a liability rather than an asset; the Americans were the only bright spot and they were not yet showing over the horizon; and finally Haig could not feel that he had the confidence of his own Political Chief.

But the British Commander-in-Chief had studied every aspect of the problem and he had the ability, the firm will, the sound judgement, acceptance of responsibility and strength of character to steer a wise course. In fact in this connection I can refer with truth and with authority to the verdict of German military opinion as quoted in the *British Official History* (*France and Belgium, 1917*), preface page v, and again in my foreword, which quotation finishes with the words, 'In the last three years of the war Haig contributed the most to prevent a German victory'. Thus he really remained MASTER OF THE FIELD.

Haig's position at this critical time was rapidly becoming more and more difficult, and the more difficult it became, the more did he exhibit all the qualities mentioned by German authority as being requisite in a great commander. Moreover it was the Prime Minister who had placed the British Army under Nivelle, an untried French General, and who had canvassed certain French generals as to their opinions on the leading British Generals, including the Commander-in-Chief himself; this hardly afforded Haig that feeling of confidence and co-operation which is so essential between the Political Chief and the General commanding the Army, especially during periods of stress and strain.

The British attack was delivered on the 9th April on the Arras-Vimy front and was completely successful not only in reaching its objectives but also in attracting the German reserves away from the French front, which was its object. The French attack, postponed on account of weather conditions, took place on the 16th April. It failed with heavy loss and little gain of ground, and it failed completely to achieve its main object which was to penetrate the German defences and destroy the principal mass of his armies. The power of the German Army had been underrated and the French had proved unfit to carry out their immense task. The question arose at once as to whether the time had not come for the release of the British from the control of the French Commander, and as to whether the instability of the French Government and the lack of success of the French armies would not cause a cessation of their operations.

On the 18th April Haig received a message to say that the Prime Minister expected to meet the French War Cabinet on the 20th and wished to know what in his (Haig's) opinion would be the effect of the French War Cabinet ordering Nivelle to cease offensive operations at an early date. Haig replied advocating a continuation of the offensive, but that the continued active co-operation of the French Army was essential.

Haig was consulted by the French authorities as well as by the British and he was even moderately probed as to Nivelle's future and who should succeed him; but he was cautious in the extreme to avoid being entangled in French politics or personalities. In the next few days Haig met Nivelle, Painlévé and Ribot at different times.

As Duff Cooper in his book on Haig, Volume II, page 97, so aptly describes the position thus:

> The irony of the situation was sublime. Two months earlier the French Government, with the enthusiastic support of the British Prime Minister, had been seeking to compel the British Commander-in-Chief to become a mere automaton under the inspired guidance of his more gifted French colleague. Now the French Minister of War was almost on his knees to that same British Commander-in-Chief to furnish him with material that might help him to get rid of that same French colleague.

Haig must have been observing the pendulum swinging in his favour—but he did not pay the least attention to that or to any personal considerations. His nature was above such pettiness. His mind was focused on the future and winning the war and to resolve the many problems, difficulties and dangers which were piling up all around him.

CHAPTER II

Conditions of the Allied Armies
—French, Russian and Italian—in 1917

O_N 1st May Haig sent a memorandum to the War Cabinet expressing his views on the new situation which was developing as a result of the failure of the French offensive, and his opinion on what steps should now be taken. This memorandum was almost identical with the proposals agreed upon subsequently at the Franco-British military conference held on the 4th May in Paris, which was attended by Haig, Robertson, Nivelle and Pétain (the latter having just been appointed Chief of the General Staff); and at which it had been agreed:

(a) that the offensive should be continued and the enemy given no respite,

(b) that the original plan, i.e. the rupture of the front, was no longer operative,

(c) that the object must now be to exhaust the enemy, and to wear down his power of resistance by attacking relentlessly with limited objectives,

(d) that the British should undertake the main operations, the French taking a secondary though active rôle,

(e) that the French should take over a portion of the British front.

On the following day, the 5th May, the Inter-Allied Conference took place in Paris at which, in addition to the four military representatives mentioned above, the two Prime Ministers, Lloyd George and Ribot, were present. The foregoing arrangements and agreements were confirmed and emphasis was laid on the following points: the immense shipping losses due to the unrestricted submarine offensive, which were threatening to endanger transport and supply, and the consequent urgency of freeing the Belgian coast—this matter was causing the British Government grave anxiety; the necessity for limiting the objectives to a distance which could be covered by our artillery and wearing down the enemy until the situation was ripe for exploitation; and lastly that the French must give full and active co-operation in offensive action which must not be left to the British single-handed.

Pétain had to report that the confidence of the French Army in its chiefs and in the Government was undermined.

The Russian and Italian situations were reviewed without any comfort or confidence.

The discussions and agreements laid the foundation of the operations for the remainder of the year 1917, influenced—and subsequently seriously so—by the deterioration of the fighting powers of our Allies—particularly of the French—who, by their self-confessed inability to protect themselves, made continuous and pressing demands for their protection by the British ally.

Two days after the Paris conference, i.e. on the 7th May, Haig convened a meeting of his Army commanders at Doullens and issued to them the outline of his plan of operations, which was as follows:

(a) the capture of the Messines-Wytschaete ridge about the 7th June as a preliminary to, and in order to secure positions from which to support,

(b) a northern operation to secure the Belgian coast by an attack on the Staden-Passchendaele-Broodseinde ridge to take place some weeks later.

He explained that the present operations would be gradually brought to a close and troops moved to the North for the purposes of (a) and (b), that the objective in the first place would be to wear down and exhaust the enemy by deliberate attacks with limited objectives, and when this end had been achieved to deliver the main blow from the Ypres front as outlined in (b).

Haig had wasted no time in setting in motion the machinery for switching his operations to the North in conformity with the situation and with the agreements reached at the Paris conference. Meanwhile news was received that serious trouble had broken out in the French Army. An infantry division had refused to go up to the front line, and signs of demoralization, such as wholesale absence without leave and refusal to obey orders, were spreading through a large number of French units.

During the following week the state of indiscipline worsened, causing intense anxiety to the French authorities. The French Government made every effort to conceal the facts.

This information rendered more difficult compliance with the instruction agreed at the Paris Conference on the 5th May to the effect that in any offensive action undertaken, the French must give full co-operation, and that such action must not be left to the British single-handed. In this connection Robertson, Chief of the Imperial General Staff, wrote to Haig on the 12th May saying that the unsettled state of affairs in France, and the probability of a separate peace with Russia, might affect the projected operations, and asked for his views.

Haig gave his views as outlined at the Army Commanders' Conference at Doullens on 7th May, but received a further letter from Robertson pointing out that the printed French version of the resolutions of the Paris Conference held on 5th May made no reference to the promise given by the French Government to continue offensive action and that this omission might mean that the French would not bind themselves to that resolution.

A further communication from Robertson by telegram added that the Prime Minister insisted on Haig's firmness regarding French co-operation in any offensive operations we undertook, and that the War Cabinet could not agree to any plan which contained the danger of our having to fight alone.

Haig immediately arranged a meeting with Pétain, who had replaced Nivelle on the 15th May. This meeting took place at Amiens on the 18th. Pétain impressed Haig; he was outspoken on the 'unrest' within the French Army, but he said he had four minor attacks in preparation—and, after studying Haig's plans, offered to co-operate in the northern offensive with six divisions (including the two at Nieuport) under General Anthoine, and agreed to take over from the British a front of 8,000 yards. He pointed out to Haig that in his opinion the objectives outlined for the northern offensive were too distant, but added that that was not his business and what was really essential was that the British Army should attack and distract the German attention from the French.

There emerged about this time some ambiguity and doubt on two matters concerning which the War Cabinet had made certain stipulations. These were:

(1) attacks when made should have limited objectives,
(2) French co-operation in any offensive was essential.

If the so-called 'unrest' in the French Army was really serious and if it should be prolonged over the operations in view, then its effect on both these stipulations would be important and indeed vital.

For example, if the mutinies were serious, then French co-operation would hardly be effective, but British offensive action would be the more necessary, or in Haig's own words, 'of more rather than less urgency.' Moreover, British offensive action might have to be prolonged over many months, in which case we should have to keep the enemy occupied with the minimum of casualties to ourselves. This would call for carefully prepared attacks with maximum of artillery power and limited objectives. Again, if the mutinies were serious, Pétain would seem to have promised more co-operation than he would be able to undertake. This promise from Pétain was passed on to the War Cabinet. But, as the official historian remarks, 'the lamentable state of the French Army completely altered the situation.'

What then was 'the lamentable state of the French Army'? Was this loss of morale, indiscipline, or mutiny, or whatever you might call it a passing phase, or was it a matter for serious concern, in fact a danger to the outcome of the war? The answer to this question was of the utmost importance to Haig and his staff.

The outbreak was undoubtedly serious, but both Nivelle and the Minister of the Interior were not unaware of the growing undercurrent. Early in 1917 tracts abounded throughout the Army, an epidemic of them, six times as numerous as three months previously. Leave-men more and more attended pacifist meetings where references were made to the greater power of Germany, the Russian revolution was glorified, and to the advocating of sabotage in munition factories. Leave-men repeated all this on their return from leave. There was open antipathy, pacifist preaching, and a campaign against national defence. Then, as Nivelle's offensive approached and spring advanced, there was a reversion in feeling, an improvement in morale, a current of optimism, a revival of hope of success. This recovery of morale was short lived, it had the effect of accentuating the moral depression which followed the failure of Nivelle's offensive after high hopes. The storm broke with some violence.

The French official account states that 119 acts of a grave character took place, of which eighty occurred between 25th May and 10th June. Then the account tabulates these and other acts which I give as follows:

Revolutionary songs and cries, stone-throwing, window-breaking, destruction of material, incendiarism, action against officers, refusal to occupy trenches, refusal to attack, cold rebellion, collective and so-called disciplined rebellion. Parallel to these acts grave incidents broke out in leave-trains—locomotives derailed, reservoirs emptied, railway employees beaten, shots fired in 119 trains, 130 railway stations in chaotic conditions, strikes and riots in the interior, and seven large towns, including Bordeaux, Nantes, Toulouse and Limoges, were the centres of serious trouble and rioting. Then follows a list of units and formations which were particularly stated to be seriously affected. The principal references were to seventy-six regiments, twenty-one battalions of chasseurs, eight regiments artillery, etc. etc. One liaison officer who regularly received direct information reported 258 battalions and eight artillery regiments as being affected. This corroborates the official French report as just stated. There were fifty-four divisions officially stated to be affected—other sources of information give sixteen army corps as seriously affected—which more or less corresponds with and corroborates the official statement of fifty-four divisions.

The *British Official History* quotes most of the foregoing. I need not repeat it, but Pétain sends his Chief of Staff, General Debeney, to Haig on 2nd June to say that, faced with this serious situation, both he and his Government considered that their one task was to nurse the French Army back to health, that the state of indiscipline in the French Army would not permit the promised Malmaison attack on the 10th June.

I repeat here the statement of Painlévé, the French War Minister at the time, that at this period there were between Soissons and Paris only two divisions on which he could confidently rely, and a memorandum written by G.Q.G. for the Minister of War on the state of the French Army at the end of September 1917 some four months later, which stated that 'any reverse would provoke anew, and this time probably beyond remedy, the dangerous crisis through which the Army had passed in May and June.'

I quote a note to page 371 of the British official account as follows:

> Marshal of the Royal Air Force Viscount Trenchard, at the time Commander of the Royal Flying Corps in France, was one of the few foreign witnesses of what he calls 'the awful demoralization of the French Army and people.' He was quartered behind the French Aisne front at various times in the summer of 1917 for reconnaissances in connection with the establishment of a base for an independent air force in an eastern area, and saw soldiers and civilians alike continually streaming back southwards along all the roads in fear of a German attack. His car was held up for six hours in a village, the road being completely blocked by a rabble of soldiers and refugees with their belongings.

This was by no means the only independent and reliable witness of the conditions, but I feel I have said enough to convince any reasonable person that the state of unrest was real, was serious and enough to create anxiety. Haig's opinion as quoted in the Official History was 'that armies do not recover from a state of serious unrest in a few weeks.' But here is a moderate statement (from a document entitled *Operations on the Western Front 1916–18, secret and confidential*) of the situation drawn up by the British Staff on the conclusion of the operations under review, and approved by Haig, which speaks for itself:

> Nivelle had led his Government and the French Army to expect so much from his spring offensive that the failure of his attack on the Aisne had a correspondingly great depressing effect on the morale of *all* in France. The French Army soon showed signs of extreme *restlessness*, and mutiny broke out here and there which developed so rapidly as to cause considerable uneasiness both at G.H.Q. and in the French Government.

18

General Pétain at once started on a mission of propaganda and during the next two months personally addressed the officers of over 100 French divisions, urging all to show greater steadfastness and to do their duty. He paid a hurried visit to Advanced G.H.Q. and begged Sir Douglas Haig to continue to attack the enemy so that the French Army might have time to recover. New regulations were also passed allowing the French soldiery ten days' leave every four months as a right. (The effect of this latter was that 350,000 French soldiers were on leave at one time as against 80,000 British.)

Thus it became increasingly evident that not only would any material assistance not be obtained from the French armies in support of the British offensive but that in their present condition the French were a source of serious anxiety in the event of any hostile offensive on their front. General Pétain was fully alive to the seriousness of the situation and in view of the condition of his troops held the view that large operations with the object of breaking through on the Western Front could obtain no decisive results and that the best plan for the remainder of the year was for the French and British to carry out small local offensives with limited objectives. He was specially desirous that the British should in no way relax their activity in order to attract and hold the German reserves and to prevent them from attacking the French. There was a further reason why it was imperative for the British to take strong and immediate action, and that was in order to prevent a concentration of troops against the Russians who were not in a position to withstand a strong offensive after their recent revolution.

The only material assistance which could be obtained from the French was the relief of the British troops as far as the River Omignon and the despatch of a small force under General Anthoine at a later date to take part in the Flanders battle. Against this must be set off the fact that the Nieuport sector was taken over by the British. In point of fact, beyond what has been stated above, no assistance was obtained from the French throughout the remainder of the year, with the exception of two local attacks, one at Verdun and the other at Fort Malmaison on the Chemin des Dames.

I naturally take it for granted that the British public realize that had the Germans gained information as to the extent and intensity of the French mutinies, they would have lost no time in attacking the French and have had no difficulty in destroying their army and compelling its surrender. I also think I can assume that the average man would realize that the British Army would then have had to fall back on the Channel ports if it could—and I don't know what eventually it would have done other than what happened in 1940 at Dunkirk. At best it would have at least presented a gloomy picture. Secrecy therefore was imperative.

The secrecy which surrounded the mutinies was something of a mystery not only at the time but for long afterwards; it was always and rightly up to a point regarded as a subject which was not to be mentioned or discussed. The *British Official History* states that 'the French Government made every effort to conceal the facts' and it certainly did so. The frontiers were effectively closed and protected from leakage, Pétain certainly exercised the iron hand in the velvet glove and used hard discipline with lenience in a dexterous manner—above all—he visited and addressed the troops of one hundred divisions concerned and did much to obscure the outward and visible signs of unrest. Clemenceau came also on the scene and he used the iron hand with vigour on all those politicians with subversive and pacifist leanings, such as the arrest of Caillaux and Malvy and members of the Bonnet Rouge; Laval was treated with no light hand and Bolo and Mata Hari were shot, while other malignants had their wings clipped or were otherwise disposed of. There are two accounts of how these troubles were handled, one is in Guedalla's *The Two Marshals*, and the other is an article which appeared in *Blackwood's Magazine* in January 1944 entitled 'The Bent Sword,' by A.M.G. (Appendix I); this gives so far as I am aware a true account.

The Australian Official Historian reports:

> The simultaneity of these outbursts, and the occurrence of several civil disturbances elsewhere in France, instantly gave rise to the suspicion that they were organized by secret and powerful defeatist agencies. For the rest of the year French politics became to a large extent a campaign for hunting down enemy agents—some real and many more suspected—in high places. There did exist at this time in the country not only many honest pacifists largely associated with pre-war syndicalist organizations, whose activities had naturally been stimulated by the Russian Revolution, but also some dangerously influential men and women who in pursuance of their own financial or other interests were engaged in intrigue countering the effort of the mass of their countrymen. Part of their endeavour was to spread a propaganda of defeatism in the press, throughout the public, and among soldiers who were daily caught and interviewed as they arrived on leave at the Parisian railway stations. . . . The diary of Sir Henry Wilson, Chief of the British Mission at Pétain's headquarters,

gives during May no hint of any true conception of the events. When Wilson began to probe the matter of French co-operation and became suspicious of the secret trouble in the French Army, his urgency became irksome and both Pétain and Foch showed him that his presence was not desired at G.Q.G., and at Pétain's request Wilson was recalled.

Very little information concerning the mutinies got through to either Switzerland or Holland; very little found its way to England and every effort was made to keep silent in the British Army, and indeed very little was known until late in 1917 and then only to a few. Robertson of course was kept informed but he also had his own means of obtaining accurate information and he was the proper channel of communication with the Government. Both Haig and Robertson were obviously fully alive to the fact that if there was any leakage to Germany or to German troops or German spies, dire results would follow and there might well have been a Dunkirk on a gigantic scale in 1917 or 1918. But Haig and Robertson were two very exceptional men, and knew how to handle this matter. They were to a considerable extent responsible for the successful maintenance of secrecy.

Haig had informed Robertson that if necessary he would suspend further operations after his assault on the Messines-Wytschaete position which was due to be delivered on 7th June, that is in five days after his receipt of information from General Debeney, Pétain's Chief of Staff, that the indiscipline was such as would not permit the promised co-operation in the form of the Malmaison attack on the 10th. Haig had the utmost confidence in his impending attack on Messines, the troops were in good heart, the preparations for the explosion of a large number of mines were complete, and indeed it would have been folly to cancel it. On his own responsibility he decided to deliver the assault. The position constituted a troublesome salient which must be reduced before any further operations in Flanders could take place.

This assault took place as arranged on 7th June and was completely successful, all objectives being gained; this achievement gave great satisfaction both in France and at home.

What is also of considerable interest to note is that the army of the German Crown Prince opposite the French was ordered to send no less than thirteen divisions of its freshest troops north for the Flanders battle which was being prepared against Prince Ruprecht's armies on the British front. The German Crown Prince was ordered to stand on the defensive and fall back if necessary. Thus, says the Official Historian, 'had the Flanders offensive cast its shadow before it.' Another satisfactory feature in the Commander-in-Chief's affairs was that the Messines-Wytschaete battle apparently had created a favourable atmosphere in London.

But with our friends the French their troubles seem to have been almost unnecessarily and inconsiderately increased by their importation earlier in the year of some 17,000 Russian soldiers who proceeded with the least possible delay to indulge in revolution on French soil, and not only that, but to infect their neighbours and preach every sort of communism, defeatism and anarchy in the country surrounding every locality in which they were quartered. These Russians were formed in three brigades, some of whom had taken part in Nivelle's recent abortive battle on the Aisne. These men had been giving serious trouble and should have been shipped back to Russia, but Russia would not have them. They started a mutiny of their own and were herded back from the front to La Cortine, situated in the middle of France, where they remained most active with their revolutionary propaganda. One brigade was of the Kerensky socialist type, one was purely Bolshevist anarchist, and one was somewhere between the two.

A gentleman named Zankievitch, representing the Kerensky provisional government, and another named Svatikoff, head of a special mission representing Kerensky personally, were charged with the task of bringing the trouble to an end. These representatives addressed the brigades on the 17th July, the Kerensky unit at Felletin with moderate success, but the Bolshevist brigade at La Cortine was no longer composed of soldiers; it had become an irresponsible political or rather anarchical horde of revolutionaries, full of complaints and hostility towards France. On the 3rd August Zankievitch ordered the 1st Bolshevist Brigade to surrender, failing which he would stop their rations, and then if they still refused to surrender he would employ the 3rd (Kerensky) Brigade to encircle the 1st Brigade and open fire not only with small arms but with artillery (*soixante-quinze* French field guns loaned by the French), the whole battle, encirclers and encircled, to be surrounded by French troops to 'keep the ring.'

By the 23rd August only fifty-seven had surrendered, the mutinous Russian troops having in the meantime dug trenches and put up barricades. Thereupon there was a concentration of French and Kerensky troops round a wide perimeter, and the civil population evacuated.

The final ultimatum to the mutineers was issued on the 14th September but with no result. On the 15th September all food was stopped and on the 16th at 10 a.m. the first gun (a French 75) was fired by the Kerensky Russians and the battle opened. The first reports stated unofficially that several thousand had been killed or wounded, but the official report which followed soon after gave the more moderate and sober figures of nine killed and forty-nine wounded. Inside the inner encirclement stood Mr Globa, the ringleader, who was made prisoner.

The Russians were then disarmed, moved to the coast, and shipped to Black Sea ports. So ended the Russian episode, but coming on top of their own troubles it gave the French authorities some anxiety and there was a good deal of communist propaganda sown in the surrounding districts. The French authorities handled this problem very carefully and cautiously, and it was only on specific and drastic instruction from Moscow that fire was opened and the trouble finally crushed.

The Messines-Wytschaete battle had, as already stated, been won, not without some mistakes, such for example as the over-crowding of our own troops on and over the final objectives. Some say also that the success should have been exploited, but I certainly disagree and Plumer and Gough were both of the same opinion. It is impossible to make no mistakes and the overcrowding was responsible for many casualties which might have been avoided. To that extent it failed to meet the require-ments of an offensive with strictly limited objectives, and seemed to confuse the intention of possible exploitation before any evidence that the conditions for exploitation were ripe. Nevertheless, it was a resounding success and put everyone in a good temper and full of hope.

To complete the picture both as regards our Allies and the enemy at approximately the middle of June 1917, it must be recorded that 'as regards Russia little was expected from their proposed offensive which, like the Izonzo battle, had been intended to synchronize with the Franco-British offensive on the Western Front. Revolutionary outbursts which had begun on the 12th March were increasing daily. A socialist group was taking charge of the policy of the Russian Government, and endeavouring to effect a peace with Germany on the basis of "no annexations." As a result of the change of government, the discipline and administration of the Russian Army had been so impaired that it seemed unlikely it would be able to continue to fight, even if so inclined.

'On the 1st July Kerensky had succeeded in inducing the more loyal units of the Russian Army to make an offensive, but after a considerable advance, chiefly against the Austrians, they were unable to withstand the German counter-attack made by the general reserve of six divisions . . . and were routed. The defeat was the signal for the Bolshevist Party to obtain control in Petrograd, and with that event Russia ceased further co-operation with the Allies in the conduct of the war.'

Our Italian allies were a constant source of anxiety, and the persistent pressure for assistance to be sent to them at the expense of the armies in France was a constant threat and danger to the conduct of the war. Towards the end of the year 1917 five British divisions and heavy artillery under the command of Plumer were sent to Italy, also a number of French divisions. The bright spot on the horizon was the American Army, but that would not begin to materialize for another year.

As regards the enemy, 'on the other hand, the political situation in Berlin reached a crisis during the month. Confidence, both in the Army and in the success of the submarine blockade of England was waning, and in addition discontent was widespread at the continued failure of the Government to state its peace terms.' Certainly in the latter half of 1917 the submarine sinkings showed some improvement, but it was still on the Belgian coast that the most dangerous submarine bases were situated and it was in this direction that the German Army would contest every inch of the ground.

The situation was confused and still further confounded by certain somewhat ambiguous stipulations laid down by the War Cabinet as regards the objectives to be aimed at, the conduct of the operations and the necessary active co-operation of the French. The very question of the objectives was difficult of explanation without disclosure of the real objective, i.e. the protection of the French from any German attack. This criticism is not intended to be directed against either the War Cabinet, the War Office or General Headquarters; it is due to the ambiguity inseparable from the peculiar factors, political, strategical, tactical and moral. There was a problem or several problems before Haig and in this connection and with him I think we must all have much sympathy and understanding.

I must not, however, anticipate the next phase of the Flanders offensive which was intended to be launched about the third week of July against the ridge or slightly elevated ground which separated Ypres from Roulers and concerning which there has been much discussion.

D

CHAPTER III

Operations in Northern Flanders
Passchendaele, First Phase—31st July to 31st August

A<small>FTER</small> the successful operation on the 7th June resulting in the capture of the Messines-Wytschaete ridge, there arose at once some misunderstanding as to what the real objective of the British Army was to be in relation to the future. Haig had, in May, told Robertson that he intended to carry out the Messines operation, and subsequently it could be decided whether to call a halt, or proceed with his projected operation in Northern Flanders with the object of freeing the Belgian coast.

There was no doubt in Haig's mind what he should do, and what he intended to do, unless he was prevented, and that was to carry on with the northern plan, capture the ridge between Ypres and Roulers, and, if he then found conditions favourable, to press forward with the object of securing the Belgian coast, including the submarine bases at Ostend and Zeebrugge.

It is important to note the steps which had been taken early in the year to draw up a plan for the Northern Flanders operation. As far back as January, in my absence owing to my projected journey to Russia, a special section of the Operations Directorate of the General Staff at G.H.Q. was set up to study, in the event of Nivelle's failure, the project of delivering such an offensive as that referred to. The plan of action was to be worked out by Colonel MacMullen with Lord Gort as his assistant. After consultation with Rawlinson (commanding 4th Army) and Plumer (commanding 2nd Army) a memorandum was submitted to Headquarters on 14th February outlining the plans of advance against the ridge east of Ypres in which (1) the final objective for the first day was to be the German second line one mile distant from the line of departure of the attack, and (2) the importance of the Gheluvelt Plateau was stressed as vital. Plumer fully concurred with this plan.

This memorandum was accepted at G.H.Q. as the official version of the Flanders plan and handed to Gough on 14th May. He, Gough, had been selected by the Commander-in-Chief to command the 5th Army which would play the leading part in the forthcoming operation. Gough took over his new front in the Ypres area on the 10th June. He held a conference of his corps commanders on the 6th June and again on the 16th June, and at these conferences of his corps commanders the plan which had been handed to him by G.H.Q. was amended and the objective, which had been limited to the German second line, a distance of one mile, was extended to include also the German third line and then the fourth line and to be continued if possible to a further objective on the main ridge at Broodseinde, with a view to exploitation.

This involved a departure from the original scheme both in principle and in detail, and in the note to page 127 of the Official History, Gough explains this and states that Haig gave him personal and verbal instructions to this effect. Immediately following Gough's conference with his corps commanders on the 16th June, Haig was called to London to attend meetings of a War Policy Committee to be held on the 19th, 20th and 21st June. (This committee comprised Lloyd George (Prime Minister), Curzon, Milner, Bonar Law and Smuts.) Haig explained his views at length, calling to mind the Cabinet Committee's resolution some eight months previously in November 1916, that there was 'no measure to which the Committee attached greater importance than the expulsion of the enemy from the Belgian coast,' that the losses in shipping in the first six months of 1917 totalled 694 Merchant Navy ships of a gross tonnage of 2,136,126 tons. He further stated that it should be possible to seize the submarine bases at Ostend and Zeebrugge, the Germans would have to stand and fight on the intervening ridge which separated Ypres from Roulers, and if he had the requisite resources in men and material he could probably advance still farther.

The Prime Minister then referred to the fact that the British would be fighting single-handed, and that he much preferred and indeed insisted on the wearing-down tactics with limited objectives, or alternatively to mount an offensive outside France against, for example, the Austrian Front. Haig rejoined with the argument that the German Army morale was showing signs of unmistakable deterioration, that he deprecated the movement of his troops to other theatres of war, and finally that he proposed in any case to follow the step-by-step tactics with limited objectives. Jellicoe restated the serious position of the shipping losses through submarine warfare, and again quoted the losses for the first six months of 1917.

The result of these meetings was that there was an inclination on the part of the Committee to leave the responsibility for decision to the military authorities on the understanding that if progress was unsatisfactory the operation as a whole would be stopped.

Haig returned to France almost immediately after the conference, and there still remained over four weeks before the offensive was due to be launched about the 25th July.

The question of the method of attack to be adopted in the forthcoming offensive and the objectives to be aimed at in the first day were obscure and in my opinion required clarification. Were the troops to penetrate as far as possible on the first day with a view to exploitation; or was the offensive to be on the step-by-step principle with limited objectives and under the support of a powerful artillery? The Commander-in-Chief had made it clear evidently to Gough that the former was the policy to adopt; and yet at the conference he informed the Prime Minister that he proposed to follow the step-by-step tactics with limited objectives, and the Official Historian says (p. 128), 'The proceedings of the War Cabinet Conference in London had a moderating influence on his outlook.' There must be some misunderstanding somewhere—probably in the definition of what was a step-by-step offensive with limited objectives.

There were certain factors governing the forthcoming operation and they appeared to be:—

(1) It had been agreed that the French could no longer give their active co-operation. General Anthoine with six divisions would take

part in the northern offensive in a small way on the extreme northern flank, and there were two minor attacks which had been postponed but might be delivered later. But there would be no effective or important co-operation.

(2) Haig had repeated many times that our intention was to wear down the enemy, but at the same time have an objective.

(3) It had been agreed that the 'wearing down' was to be achieved by short attacks with limited objectives carried out step by step within the range of powerful artillery support.

(4) The ultimate objective was to be the expulsion of the Germans from the Belgian coast and their submarine bases there.

(5) The important continuing objective was the protection of the French Army from attack by causing the attraction of the German reserves to Flanders. This would be effected by a continuation of the offensive, but probably more satisfactorily by the step-by-step method. This object could not however be advertised to the troops.

The only effective way of covering the foregoing factors, and taking a line of action which would satisfy the requirements of the Cabinet War Policy Committee, conform to the urgent appeals from Pétain and meet the requirements of Haig's strategy, would appear to be to adhere strictly and from zero hour on the first day to the principle of step-by-step carefully regulated advances to limited objectives within organized and powerful artillery range, until such a stage was reached when it would be patent that the enemy was thoroughly demoralized and exploitation could be undertaken. By this means it would be possible to inflict the maximum losses on the enemy causing damage to his morale, while reducing to a minimum our own casualties and strain on our troops.

Feeling on this matter as I did, that there was ambiguity as to what was meant by a step-by-step attack with limited objectives, and convinced that the time was not yet ripe for an 'all-out' assault, I immediately drafted a memorandum on the whole subject, determined if possible to have it adequately ventilated. In my capacity as Director of Operations at G.H.Q., I submitted this memorandum to the Chief-of-Staff, General Sir L. Kiggell, who, in agreement with me, passed it to Haig for perusal immediately on his arrival in France from the Cabinet Committee's meetings in London. Haig thereupon asked Kiggell and me to meet him the same evening to discuss the subject, and in the course of the discussion it seemed evident to me that Haig was in principle in agreement with my memorandum. I made it clear that there was ample time to amend the plan of attack as might seem desirable and that some clarification of the matter with the army commanders seemed to be necessary.

Haig at once convened a meeting at Cassel of the two army commanders concerned (5th and 2nd), Gough and Plumer, for the 28th June to discuss the subject of the memorandum, copies of which had been sent to them. The memorandum is published in full in the *British Official History, Vol. II, 1917 France and Belgium, Appendix XV*; the gist of it is stated on pages 128 and 129 of that volume to the following effect epitomized:—

That no attempt should be made to push the infantry to the maximum depth outlined in the orders; instead it advised a succession of deliberate attacks at a few days interval, limited to a depth of about a mile to which distance it had been proved without doubt that fresh troops with adequate artillery support could advance without undue loss or disorganization; artillery destructive fire on this lesser area too could be more concentrated. The memorandum pointed out that the eventual line reached, if far advanced, would probably be a ragged one from which it would be difficult for a fresh attack to start under effective barrage, or counter-attacks repulsed. By this I mean that all of the attacking troops would for example probably reach the nearest objective, some would reach a further objective, and a few would probably reach the most distant objective; this would produce a ragged, irregular front, on which an accurate immediate and previously prepared artillery barrage could not be put down to meet any hostile counter-attacks, or indeed to cover an early advance. Immediate counter-attacks by German reserves were sure to be delivered, and it would be far preferable to accept battle with those reserves when we are in an organized state, our guns in position, our troops not tired, and our communications in good state, than to engage them in some more forward position when we have none of those advantages. The memorandum expressed the belief that after a succession of effective blows, at a few days interval, the time would come when the taking of risks would be justifiable, but exploitation would not be practicable until the counter-attack divisions which the enemy could send in to the battle had been defeated and until the enemy was thoroughly demoralized. This result could not be achieved in the first day, and should not be attempted. The attacking troops would be the first to realize when the situation was ripe for exploitation and would themselves be anxious to take every advantage of it.

To put it in a nutshell, we must recognize that we were undertaking siege operations, that our first task was to blast a breach in the defences; when that had been satisfactorily achieved and the enemy sufficiently shaken and we could penetrate through the breach, then we could exploit, but not before.

The meeting which Haig convened at Cassel of the two army commanders, Gough and Plumer, to discuss the forthcoming operations in general and the memorandum (explained above) in particular took place on the 28th June. Gough had submitted a written reply to this memorandum which also forms part of Appendix XV of the Official History of the period and was published as part of that Appendix. While generally agreeing with the memorandum Gough expressed the view that it would be wasteful not to reap all the advantages possible resulting from the first day's attack; that is to say, he would advocate aiming to reach a more distant objective on the first day.

What did surprise me was the extremely definite opinion of Plumer, almost vehemently expressed to me as I walked with him to the conference room. He said, 'Do you think that after making the vast preparations for attack on this position over a long period of months, if not years, and after sitting in the salient all this time, I am going to agree to limiting the progress and advance of my troops at the outset on the first day? I say definitely *no*, I would certainly not agree to any such limitation.'

The *British Official History* confirms this view expressed to me by Plumer in the following words on page 129, 'Haig, after discussing the Davidson memorandum with him (Gough) and General Plumer at Cassel on the 28th June had with General Plumer's support allowed the 5th Army scheme to stand; it seemed perhaps worth trying an all-out attack on the first day.'

Certainly both army commanders knew that all was not well with the French Army, but possibly they did not know then the full extent of the trouble.

What puzzled me was why Plumer had gone back on his previous agreement with the original plan. I feel sure that both army commanders entered the battle on the 31st July with two objectives, or rather a double objective, to wear out *and* to penetrate, with the emphasis on the latter. This was realized at the same time by the Australian Official Historian who remarked on page 697 of his Official History:—

> The fact stands out that not only was the whole Flanders offensive planned with a largely strategical objective, but the first stroke in it was delivered, not as a closely limited battle of attrition on the lines favoured by Pétain and Robertson, but with mixed aims—to penetrate as well as to wear out. . . . Here again it by no means follows that Haig was wrong, but in this mixture of motives lay grave disadvantages.

After having heard at the conference at Cassel on the 28th both Army Commanders Gough and Plumer express their views, Haig gave his approval to the 5th Army plan and did not press the points he had raised. No alteration was made to the extended objectives, but Haig did draw attention to the necessity for strengthening the assault on the Gheluvelt Plateau, which was vital.

What must be remembered is that he had received the opinion of two army commanders very different in temperament, Plumer cautious and deliberate, Gough bold and quick-witted, and that they both took more or less the same view. It was no doubt wise that Haig should have consulted them, and having received their unanimous opinion it would not have been easy or wise to ignore it. The operation on the first day of the attack was rather exceptional as the preparation, physical and otherwise, including the construction of railway and roads, had been prolonged, especially in the case of Plumer and the 2nd Army, and one can sympathize with his anxiety to clear the Ypres salient. Haig was no doubt fully justified in taking his decision in spite of the views expressed at the recent London conference.

The continuous reports of deterioration of morale of the

German Army and people may have been exaggerated but it did definitely exist (as was proved and became obvious in later months) and doubtless this had in some degree influenced Haig to adopt a bolder course. After the conference I felt convinced that it was Plumer's unexpected and very definite and determined view and recommendation to go as far as possible on the first day that tilted the decision in this direction.

It is interesting to note that the War Cabinet withheld their sanction to the forthcoming operation and it was only on the 25th July, i.e. six days before the assault took place, that a telegram was received to the effect 'Having approved your plans being executed you may depend upon their (the Cabinet's) wholehearted support, and when they decide again to reconsider the situation they will obtain your views before arriving at any decision as to the cessation of operations.' Told by Robertson that the War Cabinet wished to know the first objective, Haig replied that it would be the ridge extending from Stirling Castle (1,200 yards E.S.E. of Hooge), by Passchendaele, Staden, Clercken to near Dixmude. There was no concealment of his proposed action.

I wish to make it perfectly clear that in submitting my memorandum my main object was to clarify the position and ensure that the assault should take place with a clear and agreed understanding. I did not dissociate myself with the decision taken, and make no claim to have supported any other alternative. I put the alternative in the strongest way I could in order to ensure mature consideration and this object was achieved. The decision was the responsibility of the Commander-in-Chief wholeheartedly supported by his two army commanders. When, owing to various causes, he found that the situation was developing unsatisfactorily he with commendable speed reversed the whole plan and put the alternative plan into immediate operation, as we shall see, with consummate skill and immediate success.

The artillery preparation commenced on the 16th July and the date fixed for launching the attack was the 25th July. Unfortunately General Anthoine and his six French divisions which were to be on the extreme northen flank arrrived late and his artillery arrived still later, and in consequence the assault had to be delayed for six days, i.e. to the 31st July. On that very day the weather broke and rain begain to fall, continued almost without cessation for three days and rendered much of the ground almost impassable. In spite of the fact that Haig had ordered 7,000 men to be sent to Anthoine to help to get his artillery into position, the delay persisted. If the assault had been able to take place on the 25th July as planned, there would have been six fine dry days which would have been of inestimable benefit and made all the difference, but as it was, the assault coincided with the break in the weather. Haig was the subject of extreme misfortune in this respect. The effect of the six days' delay was that there were six extra days' bombardment which increased the destruction of the ground, and the rain filled the shell holes and created a wide band of churned-up mud and water.*

The troops advanced to the assault on the morning of the 31st July and the result of the battle by the evening was satisfactory up to a point, but only relatively so. Nine of the enemy's divisions had been badly shattered and had to be replaced within a few days, there were an unusually large number of dead on the battlefield, and some 6,000 prisoners had been taken. A steady stream of German reserves to Flanders began as a result

* In Sir James Edmonds' (late Official Historian) book entitled *A Short History of World War I*, published in 1951, it is stated on page 245:

'Many delays occurred in the launching of the new campaign . . . so that the enemy was given six weeks to arrange counter measures. Gough, having different ideas from Plumer, required alterations made in the staging of the battle.'

And again on page 252 it is stated:

'Had it not been for the two unfortunate postponements due to Plumer's preparations not suiting Gough's ideas, and later Gough's preparations not suiting Plumer's, fine weather being wasted in each instance, a greater success would have been achieved at less cost.'

Not understanding what these statements meant, I applied for an explanation to Sir James Edmonds, who replied that he was going to issue a notice of correction.

In fact after the clarification of the objectives at the conference held at Cassel on the 28th June, no difference of opinion as between the two army commanders occurred involving delay, and in the succeeding four weeks between 29th June and the 26th July there was nothing to require any postponement of the assault except the late arrival of the French contingent and their heavy artillery, which were given every help, including some thousands of the British Labour Corps, to assist them in installing their guns.

of this day's fighting and this was to continue and draw off the enemy's resources from the French front.

The day's objectives had, however, not been reached and the line occupied was ragged. A heavy counter-attack threatened at midday, but the artillery did not know the exact line which had been gained, forward artillery observers lost touch with the batteries, and observers along the second objective could not see what was ahead. In places the line reached in the morning was held, but in other places had to give way. The nine leading divisions of the 5th Army were less than halfway to the first day's objectives, and the situation of the 2nd Corps opposite Gheluvelt was unsatisfactory. This corps was ordered to attack next day, but a memorandum sent by the Operation Branch G.H.Q., written for Haig, recommended that the attack should not be hurried, that it should be carried out by two fresh divisions after at least two or three days' artillery preparation. The recommendations were accepted. The Gheluvelt plateau was vital to the whole battle. Weather conditions were bad and the sodden ground was churned into a bog—duckboard tracks and plank roads had to be laid for purposes of supply. The physical hardships and mental strain on the troops were severe.

The battle lasted on and off for about four weeks, held up periodically by wet and stormy weather. A further effort was made to secure the Gheluvelt Plateau and proved to be a failure. There were minor and piecemeal attacks here and there to rectify and improve positions; these were for the most part costly, exhausting and ineffective; while some succeeded, others failed, but no great progress had been made during these four weeks after the initial attack. I refer to this whole period as the Passchendaele Operations First Phase.

I now quote from the *Australian Official History*:—

From early in August the question whether the battle was being fought on right lines was still deeply concerning the staff at G.H.Q. and Haig circulated to all his Army commanders on 7th August a second, admirably lucid appreciation prepared by it, in which the question was again raised whether the objectives that had been set for 31st July were not too extensive. It was pointed out that the objective of the present offensive in its early stages was not to break through the Germans, but to wear them down. Should not the depth of the objectives be limited by consideration not merely of the range of the artillery, but of the training, discipline, and bodily strength of the infantry? Should not the objective be near enough for the troops to reach it in good order and without fatigue, so that they could resist the counter-attack and prepare quickly for the next advance?

This paper drew another remarkably clear appreciation, this time from General Rawlinson. He pointed out that the British Command had never yet attempted to conduct a wearing-down battle with planned, logical methods, but had relied too much on its belief that a breakdown of the German Army's morale was within sight.

Rawlinson's appreciation is also quoted as follows:—

We have never yet set ourselves deliberately to carry out a battle of attrition on absolutely definite lines, with successive objectives well within covering range of the artillery, and well within the physical capacity of the infantry. We have never issued hard-and-fast orders that these objectives are not to be exceeded, however easily they may be gained. We have never set ourselves to work to deliver a succession of carefully worked out hammer blows on the enemy at short intervals with the object of definitely beating him to his knees, so that there is no question that his morale is finally broken. Then, and not till then, shall we be able to take liberties. When that stage is reached moreover we shall know it instinctively. It will not be a matter of conjecture built up on reports of prisoners and deserters. It will be an established fact known to every man in our own as well as the enemy's ranks.

I again quote from the Australian Official Historian two short paragraphs in summing up this first phase of four weeks:—

He says in relation to the series of actions or attainments (as he calls them) that except for the first, i.e. that of the 31st July, they were 'really insignificant in every result but that of exhausting possibly both sides, certainly the British.'

Again he says, 'The truth was that these strokes, aimed at the morale of the German Army, were wearing down the morale of the British.'

I shall have a great deal more to say about the morale of both sides later on in these notes.

I must now relate the remarks of the British Official Historian on the result of the four weeks' fighting, 31st July to 28th August:—

The casualties during the four weeks of August (31st July–28th August) since the opening day of the main offensive had amounted to 3,424 officers and 64,586 other ranks. . . . In all 22 British Divisions (including one twice) had been engaged on the Fifth Army front, of which fourteen had been relieved and withdrawn to refit. . . . The casualties alone do not give the full picture of the situation; for, apart from actual losses, the discomfort of the living conditions in the forward areas and the strain of fighting with indifferent success had overwrought and discouraged all ranks more than any other operation fought by British troops in the war, so that, although the health of the troops did not suffer, discontent was general: the soldier hates discomfort more than he fears danger. The memory of this August fighting, with its heavy showers, rain-filled craters and slippery mud, was as deeply impressed on the combatants who could not be told the reason for the Commander-in-Chief's persistency, and such stories of it were spread at home by the wounded, that it has remained the image and symbol of the whole battle, overshadowing the subsequent successful actions of the campaign and preventing the true estimation of them, even in some cases stopping any knowledge of them reaching the public ear.

The Historian goes on to say:—

The credit side of the balance sheet, even at this stage, was not inconsiderable. During the period 25th July to 28th August, 23 German Divisions (17 in the first three weeks) had been exhausted and withdrawn out of the 30 which had been engaged (two of them twice) opposite the Fifth Army alone and . . . . Northward 7 more with heavy losses opposite to the French First Army. Of this total of 37 Divisions—as against 26 Allied (4 French and 22 British) Divisions—9 had come from Champagne and Alsace-Lorraine, thereby relieving anxiety in that direction; information, too, had been received by G.H.Q. of a diminution of 70 per cent. in the German heavy gun ammunition in the French sector, indicating that the Germans had had to concentrate their available heavy artillery ammunition in Flanders. More important than this, Sir Douglas Haig's purpose to draw all available German reserves to the British sector was proving effective. The French battlefront had been left unmolested and German plans for the attack on the Russian Front had had to be postponed.

As regards the French, the Official History states that at this time

although the French Army was showing signs of recovery under Pétain's careful handling, a small German attack upset the preparations which had been made for an offensive on a wide front at Verdun to synchronize with the opening stage of the Northern Operations in Flanders (i.e. on the 31st July) and caused its postponement (till the 20th August) so that for the moment the prospect of French assistance faded out.

Although there may have been and probably were some superficial indications of partial recovery in the French Army, they were superficial and evidenced by a more docile and obedient attitude, but the conditions were still serious and there was no will to fight, either offensively or defensively. The greater part of the Army was not reliable and could not be depended upon. When General Anthoine, Commander of the 1st French Army, visited Haig before the opening of the Northern Flanders offensive he brought a message from General Pétain: 'L'offensive des Flandres doit être assuré d'un succes absolu, *imperiousement exigé par des facteurs moraux du moment.*' (Italicized in original.) This also gives the direct answer to those who say that Pétain was opposed to the Flanders offensive.

I shall have much to say later about the French Army and will leave it at the moment with the simple remark that if the Germans had put up an attack of even a few divisions they would have had at that time no difficulty in walking through the French defences. I leave the reader to imagine what the result of that would have been.

As to the Russians their Army was in a state of disintegration; the Germans had crushed the Kerensky offensive in July and were shortly to break the Russian front at Riga. The Russians were on the road to Brest-Litovsk as the Italians were on the road to Caporetto.

And now for the Germans—what was the opinion of our enemy on the four weeks of the first phase beginning on 31st July. Ludendorf writes,

> On 31st July the fighting cost us very heavy losses in prisoners and stores and a large expenditure of reserves; and the costly August battles imposed a great strain on the Western troops. I myself was being placed in an awkward predicament. The state of affairs in the West appeared to prevent the execution of our plans elsewhere, our wastage had been so high as to cause grave misgivings and exceed all our expectations.

Ludendorf also adds:

> From the 31st July 1917 till well into September was a period of tremendous anxiety, the fighting on the Western front became more serious than any the German Army had yet experienced.

Von Kuhl, after stating that conditions were much worse on their (the German) side, and the toll of sickness very heavy, goes on to add 'the Hell of Verdun was surpassed. The Flanders battle was called the Greatest Martyrdom of the World

War. There were no trenches and no shelters except the few concrete block-houses; in the water-filled craters cowered the defenders without shelter from weather, hungry and cold, abandoned without pause to overwhelming artillery fire.'

Such were the official views of the combatant countries; undoubtedly the casualties were heavy, and the strain on the troops and the hardships were almost unbearable on both sides. I feel that the consensus of opinion would be that the operations should have been conducted from the outset on the step-by-step principle, with a heavy concentration of force against the key position known as the Gheluvelt Plateau.

That a more ambitious and far-reaching plan was recommended and approved was no doubt due to the anxiety of both army commanders and the Commander-in-Chief to take advantage of the prolonged and immense preparations and concentration of power, to strike as far as possible on the first day and inflict the maximum punishment on the enemy. This was in line with the instinctive feeling of Haig that German morale, both among the civil population and the German Army, was at least beginning to be affected and he sensed the importance of striking and striking hard. The postal evidence in Germany showed the growing feeling of strain and weariness, if not discontent, of the soldiery in their letters home, and it is to be noted that the Reichstag on the 19th July by 214 votes to 133 passed a resolution demanding a peace by negotiation. German soldiers are naturally tough and highly disciplined, and it would take a good deal of loss of morale and confidence to affect their soldierly qualities in the field. But as I have already said this subject of morale will receive my attention later on.

Another factor which concerned the commanders was that the amphibious operation which was being prepared under Rawlinson on the sea coast was awaiting the advance of the Flanders Army, and if the next high tide required for landing purposes was missed, it would have to wait for another four weeks, causing it to be launched very late in the season.

About the third week in August Haig, with commendable decision, reaching the conclusion that the operations were getting on to wrong lines and leading nowhere, took immediate steps to terminate them. He got to work without loss of time to change the whole method and tactical principle. He transferred the main task, including the responsibility for the capture of the Gheluvelt Plateau and the ridge beyond it, to Plumer, and instructed him to work on the principle of advancing step by step with limited objectives and overwhelming artillery power, in short in accordance with the procedure which had been advocated earlier.

There was no delay about this changeover, when Haig made the decision he put the machinery into gear immediately. This ushered in the second phase of the Passchendaele operations, commencing on the 28th August and which lasted five weeks. In my opinion this second phase, which follows, constitutes the turning point when we were getting the upper hand, but which was recognized by hardly anyone at the time.

In the first phase we had shaken the enemy, but we had at the same time shaken ourselves substantially; in the next phase we damaged the enemy's morale and at the same time raised our own.

CHAPTER IV

Operations in Northern Flanders
Passchendaele, Second Phase—1st September to 7th October

O<small>N</small> the 21st August Haig reported the situation to the War Cabinet, stating that he was satisfied with the recent operations and that, if it had not been for the adverse weather conditions, he would have been able to make much more progress. He laid stress on the heavy wastage of the enemy, he anticipated considerable results in the near future, and expressed his opinion that 'the right course to pursue is undoubtedly to press the enemy in Flanders without intermission and to the full extent of our power.'

The third effort to gain ground on the Gheluvelt Plateau having failed on 24th August and being reported to G.H.Q. the same afternoon, Haig decided at once to suspend operations for the moment and change the plan, transferring the principal role from the 5th to the 2nd Army. On the 25th he visited Plumer in the morning and, informing him of the recent failure and restating the importance of the Gheluvelt Plateau, he announced his intention to concentrate his maximum effort for its capture and, owing to the desirability of having the operation under one command, he proposed to place it under the command of Plumer and transfer the 2nd Corps and its frontage from the 5th to the 2nd Army. He asked Plumer to make immediate preparation for this, which should take the form of a succession of attacks at intervals of a few days with strictly limited objectives and within range of a powerful artillery until the Zandvoorde–Polygon Wood–Broodseinde position had been gained.

Haig held a conference later the same day, the 25th August, at G.H.Q., at which both Plumer and Gough were present. He

41

E

explained the new scheme and it was agreed to transfer the 2nd Corps front to Plumer on the 1st September. Plumer asked for three weeks to make his preparations and this was agreed. The 5th Army was instructed to continue to be active but, after an abortive and costly further effort on certain tactical features on the plateau on the 27th which had no result except to inflict a further strain on the troops in appalling weather, all further activities, except for certain minor engagements, ceased.

Haig reported again to the War Cabinet on the 2nd September and explained and regretted that there would be a delay of three weeks in the resumption of operations till the third week in September and, at the same time, reported the shortage of artillery ammunition. He also repeated his conviction that 'the best, if not the only, way to surmount the crisis and the temporary inaction of the French Army was to continue the campaign with all available resources.'

It must be remembered that the Cabinet Committee, when reviewing the situation at its meetings on the 19th to 21st June, which Haig attended, after much deliberation had decided to let the Northern Flanders operation proceed, but made the reservation that if at any time the results appeared to be unsatisfactory, the situation would be reviewed and, if considered advisable, the operation would be suspended.

A conference was held in London on the 4th September which Haig attended. Mr Lloyd George returned to his previous arguments that as the British were fighting virtually alone, the Russians being practically out of it, the French unable to take any active part, and the Italians calling for assistance in heavy artillery, it would be better for us to conserve our energy and resources during the remainder of 1917 and only undertake minor operations such as the support of the Italians against Austria. Haig answered this as he had done on previous occasions, namely, expressing his 'conviction that to withdraw a single man or gun from Flanders, or from the Western Front, would be a most unsound policy.' In his opinion, the Prime Minister's proposal to sit still for the remainder of 1917 would give the enemy the initiative and allow him to strike a blow at one or other of the Allies, which might prove disastrous. From a military point of view it was preferable to fight the Germans on ground where the British armies were already established with their supply services intact and close to the coast, than to be forced to send divisions hurriedly to support a tottering French or Italian battle.

The majority of the Cabinet, after discussion, were in favour of letting the operations in Northern Flanders continue, and Haig gave way to the extent of agreeing to consult Pétain regarding the despatch of some more heavy artillery to Italy.

Haig's two chief anxieties at that time were the possibility of bad weather and mud necessitating the closing of the Flanders operations and the switch of troops and guns to other parts of the British front, and, secondly, a communication from Robertson that the drafts for September would do no more than replace normal wastage. As regards the first, a memorandum by Operations G.H.Q. made recommendations for switches to certain selected fronts in case of need. On the 16th September Byng, commanding 3rd Army, produced details of his projected operation with tanks in front of Cambrai. Haig thought well of the Cambrai scheme and promised his support to it, if possible.

Throughout these deliberations, Haig's chief concern was to divert German attention, particularly from the French front. The limited French attack at Verdun, promised by General Pétain on the 2nd June for the end of July, had indeed, as we have seen, been carried out at the end of August; but within four weeks, on the 19th September, the French Commander-in-Chief was again imploring that the offensive in Flanders should be continued without further delay. During this special visit to British Headquarters he assured Haig that between the British right and Switzerland he had not a man on whom he could rely. Not only, he said, had the French Army ceased to be able to make any considerable offensive, but its discipline was still so bad that it would be unable to resist a determined German offensive. France was nearing the limit of her man-power and the danger existed that the French Government would—as indeed G.H.Q. had feared in the two preceding winters—demand a separate peace rather than withstand

43

another German offensive and its resulting casualties. Even after making allowance for General Pétain's pessimistic outlook, Haig appreciated the urgency of his repeated requests for a breathing space for the recovery of the French Army. The imperative need to retain France as an active partner in the war was evident and her decision on this vital matter had become the dominant factor in the situation.

It is interesting to note here that on page 236 of the *British Official History* it is stated that with a general reserve of no more than six divisions thrown in, the Germans crushed the Kerensky offensive in July, were to break the Russian front at Riga (1st–5th September) and the Italian front at Caporetto (24th October). It gives one to think what would have happened if they had attacked the French front, but they were prevented from doing so by the British Army. It is also instructive to find a memorandum written by the French Headquarters for the Minister of War on the state of the French Army at the end of September 1917 which stated that 'any reverse would provoke anew, and this time probably beyond remedy, the dangerous crisis through which the Army had passed in May and June.' I have quoted this before, but I deliberately quote it again to reinforce my argument that we could not plead that we had not been warned, nor could we plead that the warning was not justified.

As a result of the firmer control adopted by Haig after 24th August, effect was given to his own advice to Gough two months earlier that the main battle of the campaign should be fought on and for Gheluvelt Plateau. Although the general plan remained unaltered the tactical scheme was radically revised. The fullest possible weight of the 2nd Army was to be massed against the plateau, the occupation of which was to be carried out by a succession of assaults, or steps as they were called, with strictly limited objectives. The 2nd Army, operating against the Gheluvelt Plateau on higher ground, would cover the advance of the 5th Army to the north on its left and on lower ground. Thus the two armies would proceed by a succession of steps to secure the Staden–Passchendaele Ridge which constituted the watershed between Ypres and Roulers.

Plumer submitted his scheme to G.H.Q. on the 29th August and, with some slight amendment, it was approved. The plan was to capture the plateau in four separate steps at six days' interval between each. The first step was timed to take place on 20th September. Two corps were to be employed to carry out the assault; each corps would have two attacking divisions, and each division attacking would have a front of 1,000 yards, making 4,000 yards as the total front of the two corps. The depth of the attack to the final objective was 1,500 yards. This limited distance was due to the necessity of meeting enemy counter-attacks with reasonably fresh infantry, of avoiding a ragged line on the objective, and of securing an accurate and effective artillery barrage. Great importance was attached to the action of the artillery and the concentration of fire on definite targets and hostile battery positions, in addition to the formal barrages covering either attack or defence. Reserves to meet enemy counter-attacks were to be echeloned in depth to the rear. An immense amount of work was required to be done in connection with communications, signals, transport, traffic, light railways, etc., as well as the accumulation of ammunition on a very large scale.

Compared with the assault on the 31st July, double the force was to be employed against the Gheluvelt Plateau to cover half the frontage of attack. The preparations were indeed almost comparable to those required for siege operations on a large scale. A feature, and a very important one, in the arrangements for the attack was that provision should be made for rapid if not immediate relief of the infantry carrying out the assaults. This was particularly appreciated by the troops and saved undue exhaustion. Over 12,000 men of the Labour Corps assisted the Engineers in their task of road and track construction.

To attempt any description of the immense preparations for the battle and their execution is outside the scope of these notes. The *Official History, Vol. II, 1917*, relates them in an admirable and most interesting manner. There is no doubt that Plumer and his Chief of Staff, Harrington, left nothing to chance; everything appeared to be thought of and weighed.

The two corps which would carry out the attack were the

10th Corps and the 1st Anzac Corps, with the 2nd Anzac Corps in reserve for use in later fighting. The southern flank was to be guarded by the 19th Division of the 9th Corps, and the remaining seven miles of the 2nd Army frontage southwards were to be occupied defensively with the least possible force consistent with safety. On the other, northern, flank would be the 5th Army, which would advance with its right covered by the assault on the plateau.

The attack was launched at daybreak on the 20th September under a barrage by the artillery of a depth of a thousand yards and of an extent and weight beyond all precedent. Thus, together with the machine-gun barrage, which lay between the heavy and field-gun barrages, five belts of fire, each accountable for two hundred yards in depth, preceded the infantry. I must now quote the British Official Historian, who gives a graphic description of the advance:—

> Massively supported in this manner, it is no wonder that the four assaulting Divisions advanced with the utmost resolution. The three sunny weeks of September had hardened the ground between the shell craters, and, although it was slippery after the night's rain, the Infantry were able to pick their way and generally keep pace with the Artillery timetable. The barrage, described by eye witnesses as magnificent both in accuracy and volume, covered the first two hundred yards rapidly in lifts of 50 yards every two minutes, and, in an initial rush the Infantry, following within two hundred yards of or closer to the barrage, took the German outposts and local counter-attack groups by surprise. Overrun in the mist, many parties were caught in their shelters, or on the point of emerging from them, and both hand grenades and inflammatory phosphorous bombs proved most useful for clearing dug-outs and shelters and forcing a quick surrender. The pace of the barrage then slowed to lifts of 100 yards every six minutes and the rate of fire of the Field Batteries was halved to two rounds a gun a minute.
>
> The western half of the plateau was soon covered with small assault groups worming their way in single file between the shell craters into the German defence system. In general, unnerved and stunned by the concentrated blast of the heavy high-explosive shell in the two forward belts of the barrage, many of the Germans in the front line, and even in more distant lines, were completely demoralized. Although only a few of the concrete shelters and pillboxes had been smashed by direct hits, and many of the machine gun emplacements had escaped destruction, their occupants were found dazed and inactive, gunners sitting beside their unfired guns. Those who were still capable of action had but the one idea, to

surrender as soon as possible, and ran forward waving handkerchiefs and pieces of white bandage to meet the approaching Infantry. On the few occasions when opposition was encountered the mist helped the attacking troops to pass round the flanks, whilst the new attack organization, especially the immediate use of the local reserves, maintained the forward impetus, although frequently at high cost in casualties in the few places where a strong resistance was offered.

The assault was made in three bounds with a halt at the completion of the first and second for purposes of mopping up and the defence consolidated. The principle of the German defence was to launch counter-attacks for which three German divisions were in reserve. Local counter-attacks by reserve battalions of the enemy's front line regiments to regain lost ground were delivered in the morning, but were everywhere repulsed. In the afternoon the heavier counter-attacks were delivered from the reserve divisions but the heavy barrages put down by our artillery created havoc amongst the attacking Germans. The S.O.S. calls for these barrages were answered almost instantaneously by our artillery and the result was devastating. An Australian officer said afterwards that his men south of Polygon Wood simply sat back and laughed when they saw the opportunity they had been waiting for snatched away by the guns; they knew that the Germans would be unable to pass through such a barrage and, in fact, no further sign of movement was seen that evening.

All enemy counter-attacks, and there were several of them, were completely smashed by the barrages, the effect of which was stated to be 'beyond description,' and the enemy stampeded. This applied to both 2nd and 5th Armies. The whole objective of both armies had been gained and held except for the strong points at Tower Hamlets on the extreme right.

The British Official Historian sums up:—

> Thus ended with complete success, except at Tower Hamlets, the first step in Sir Douglas Haig's first trial of step-by-step advance; the much-vaunted new German defence tactics had failed to stop the new method. The change was not appreciated in England or in France and the success was underrated by the public, but not by the troops themselves or by their adversaries.

> Within seventy-two hours of the substantial capture of the final objective on the 20th September, all the six Divisions which had made

the main assault, those of the X Corps and I Anzac Corps of the Second Army and the V Corps of the Fifth Army, had been relieved by the Divisions in close reserve.

The general opinion of the troops was that if every attack could be carried out so cleanly and be followed by relief so quickly, the men would be well content. During the period of the assault and counter-attacks, 3,243 prisoners had been taken, and very heavy losses in killed and wounded, in addition to the capture of a quantity of booty; but the outstanding gain was that the Germans had been driven from the major part of their key position on the Gheluvelt plateau.

In the sector of the 23rd Division alone, astride the Menin Road, over a thousand German dead were buried within the British lines.

I must quote what the Australian Official Historian has to say in summing up the results of this day's operation, namely, the first step of the series of step-by-step advances with limited objectives, known as the Menin Road Battle, 20th September, and part of the Passchendaele second phase.

So ended, with complete success, the first step in Haig's trial of true step-by-step tactics; the British Army did precisely what it was intended to do, and did it even more cleanly than it did at Messines. The objectives being easily within the capacity of the troops, there were few 'ragged edges'; only two local British counter-attacks were launched afterwards, one at Hill 37 by the 55th Division which succeeded, and one at Tower Hamlets by the 41st Division which failed. The fact that the Germans were well prepared and had their counter-attack Divisions ready was actually an advantage. The more the enemy thrust his reserves under that crushing barrage the better, for practically none of them came through. Although German historians still assert that the British attack was in some way brought to a stop by the German counter-attack, the movements actually made by the counter-attack Divisions were in most parts not counter-attacks at all but costly efforts to reach the positions to which the line divisions had been driven back. Not only did none of the counter-attack troops reach the Australian Infantry, but their effort could barely even be detected by it. The German Command would have secured the same result at far less cost if it had used the storm divisions merely to relieve the remnant of the line divisions after dark. The fact stands out that the Allies were now using their superiority in material in a way which, granted fine weather, made success certain.

This historian goes on to say that the German troops came out of the battle crushed and the British comparatively fresh. The German official account says: 'the new English method of attack had proved its effectiveness.'

48

The Australian goes on to add:—

This success differed from all others in which Australians had yet participated in that it was part of a well-planned series of operations leading definitely towards victory in the war. But, though it caused some rejoicing in England and France, its real importance was probably under-rated there; earlier failures had caused the people to be cautious and the Governments sceptical.

The first step had been executed with precision and with great satisfaction to all ranks, even to the most critical; great encouragement was given to the rank and file and especially was it satisfactory to hear reports that the operation had had an inspiriting effect on the infantry and provided an effective tonic on morale generally. Reports on the other hand were received of the opposite effect on the enemy, especially among the prisoners captured, but that is no sure sign, for depression usually accompanies capture.

The artillery began to make the forward move on the after-noon of the 20th and, on the following morning, 21st September, Haig issued his instructions for the execution of the second step across the Gheluvelt Plateau in accordance with the plan already drawn up by Plumer and approved. The objective in this step was roughly at a distance of 1,200 yards, and was to include the whole of the Polygon Wood and the greater part of Zonnebeke village. The divisional front of attack was again 1,000 yards and the forthcoming assault was scheduled for the 26th September, and the artillery moved forward to their new positions. All preparatory steps were taken as before, communi-cations repaired for the movement of ammunition, guns and supplies. The weather was dry and the ground hard and dusty.

Unfortunately, on the 25th, the day preceding the attack, the Germans launched a well-directed, powerful and determined counter-attack between the Menin Road and the edge of Polygon Wood, with the object of threatening the flank of our projected attack which had been anticipated, and weakening our hold on the Gheluvelt Plateau. Some units of the 33rd Division were driven back a short distance, and exposed the southern flank of the Australians holding the edge of Polygon Wood. The situation in that area became confused and created anxiety lest it should interfere with the main attack next morning. It was largely due to the efficient handling and determination of the 15th Australian Brigade that the danger was averted, so that the main attack of the Anzac division concerned was enabled to carry through with its assault next day as originally planned and with complete success.

I will not refer in any detail to the progress of the battle of the 26th. Practically the whole of the objectives were captured punctually along the whole of the front of the attack. The feature of this action was the number of counter-attacks which were delivered by the Germans during the course of the day, all of which were heavily defeated. These counter-attacks had been anticipated and the preparations to meet them, especially on the part of the artillery, were conspicuously effective. Local hostile counter-attacks by local reserves were delivered at various points in the morning, and the more serious attacks took place by the divisions in reserve in the afternoon. Nowhere did the enemy succeed in recovering any of the ground he had lost. Frequent reports of the progress of the counter-attacks from air and ground observers were quickly and accurately received by our artillery, whose barrages crashed almost instantaneously with devastating effect on the enemy advancing. The task of our artillery proved on this occasion more arduous and costly, as the German artillery had been reinforced to support the counter-attack delivered on the previous day.

A larger number of German divisions had been used in this battle of the 26th than in that of the 20th, both to support their front divisions and for counter-attack purposes and none had achieved its purpose in any instance, but all had been subjected to very severe losses.

The objective of this, the second step, known as the Polygon Wood Battle of the 26th September, had not only been gained and held, but the destruction of the German reserve divisions was being carried out faster and in larger number. The general effect on our troops was similar to that on the 20th September, a feeling of superiority over the Germans which, as a result of the two battles, Menin Road on the 20th and Polygon Wood on the 26th, was growing.

The outstanding success of the first two steps and the rapid wastage of the enemy's reserve divisions led Haig to give serious consideration to the prospect of early exploitation. The next step was due to take place on the 4th October and was designed to capture Broodseinde on the top of the ridge, and Haig, at a conference with Plumer and Gough on 28th September, informed them that his intention after the next step was to press the attack deeper and seize any opportunity for exploitation for which preparation should be made beforehand. He spoke of holding fresh reserves ready to push through, supported by artillery, cavalry and tanks. He asked the two army commanders for their requirements. They both complied with this request but both, independently, in covering letters expressed the view that extensive exploitation would be premature before the main Passchendaele–Westroosebeke Ridge had been secured, which would necessitate two additional steps and a pause for restoration of communications and supplies. Haig replied to these queries that his instructions to his army commanders were to be ready to take advantage of any opportunity which might present itself, and referred to the loss of opportunity by the Germans on 31st October 1914, when the British in the Ypres salient were exhausted after repeated attacks made on them.

A further conference was held by Haig with the two army commanders on the 2nd October. The arrangements for exploitation were not to be applicable to the third step, due on 4th October to reach Broodseinde, but for the subsequent attack due about the 10th October if conditions were suitable. They were described in greater detail both strategically and tactically, as well as administratively, and were agreed upon by both army commanders as consequent on any outstanding success on that later date.

The plan of assault for the 4th October was as follows: 1st Anzac Corps to capture Broodseinde on a front of 2,000 yards astride the Moorslede Road; the 2nd Anzac Corps to capture the Gravenstafel spur on a front of 3,000 yards; 5th Army to attack on the left towards Poelcapelle with four divisions left on the Ypres–Staden Railway, the right flank to be protected by the 10th Corps advancing 1,200 yards to the eastern edge of the Gheluvelt Plateau.

An extraordinary and somewhat disturbing feature presented itself on the morning of the 4th October, which ultimately turned out to our advantage. At 5.20 a.m. the German artillery barrage opened on the front of the 1st and 2nd Australian Divisions causing casualties and presaging an attack which turned out to have been timed exactly with the assault of the British, viz., 6 a.m. The Australians, under their own barrage, chased the Germans back, killing many and taking many prisoners.

The result of this third step was that the whole of the objectives were gained along the whole front of both armies, including Broodseinde and Gravenstafel. The success was complete and, as anticipated, it at first appeared to open up many possibilities. As the Australian Official Historian relates and as the British Official Historian repeats: 'An overwhelming blow had been struck and both sides knew it'.

It will be as well to quote the authoritative comments of all four official historians who represented respectively the countries whose troops took part in the battle, namely, Great Britain, Australia, New Zealand and Germany.

Brigadier-General Sir James Edmonds, the British Official Historian, regarding this battle of 4th October writes:—

> The main objectives had been gained and the number of prisoners was exceptionally large, the Second Army alone having taken over 4,000. In the opinion of officers of long experience on the Western front, the number of dead Germans seen on the battlefield exceeded that observed in any previous assault of the war, and messages stressed the demoralized state of the survivors.

Here is the report of the Australian Official Historian, Dr C. E. W. Bean:—

> The objective was the most important yet attacked by the Second and Fifth Armies, and they had again done exactly what they had planned to do. The recent German decision to hold the front line in greater strength had merely resulted in the destruction of the troops placed there. The German staffs waiting on Broodseinde ridge for news of the success of their own enterprise at Zonnebeke had found their attack troops swept away, and the wave engulfing themselves. The subsequent throwing of two

counter-attack divisions against the Anzac front failed to regain an inch of ground. The Anzac troops, despite the intense fire laid on them from the start, had never fought better. This was the third blow struck at Ypres in fifteen days with complete success. It drove the Germans from one of the most important positions on the Western Front; notwithstanding their full knowledge that it was coming, they were completely powerless to withstand it. As regards merely the extent of front and the forces engaged, it was no greater operation than Messines, which also was comparable to it in the cleanness of the result. But coming on top of the achievements of September 20th and 26th, its success was of an entirely different order—'The black day of October 4th' as the German Official History calls it. Ludendorf says that the battle 'was extraordinarily severe and again we only came through it with enormous losses.' No Army could continue to withstand such blows. These clean victories on comparatively wide fronts were in sharp contrast with the uneven successes of the First Somme. It is true that the British loss also, at least in the two Anzac Corps, was severe. The Germans had fought hard; the spirit of many of their Divisions was still stubborn. But the German Command had this day barely been able to supply the reserves required, and the reserves when thrown in had been far less effective than their Commanders realized. One or two more such strokes, and, with proper provision beforehand, even 'exploitation' might be attempted with confidence. The success of those strokes could be made a certainty provided good weather continued. Granted this condition, there was little doubt that the Commanders could at last powerfully affect, if not decide, the issue of the war.

It was this fact that differentiated the battle of Broodseinde from all previous victories in which the Australians had participated in France, and even from the battle of Arras, in which the first stroke was perhaps more stunning, but subsequent success was never really on the horizon. It is true that, as before, the British and French people, and even their Governments, recognized only another of the victories they had heard shouted so often. . . . Yet among many well-informed observers at the front there was a definite feeling that this battle was the most complete success so far won by the British Army in France. The fact that the condition necessary to the consummation of the step-by-step campaign—good weather—was improbable makes no difference to the import of the battle of Broodseinde. For the first time in years, at noon on October 4th on the heights east of Ypres, British troops on the Western Front stood face to face with the possibility of decisive success.

Here follows the report of the New Zealand Official Historian (Stewart):—

Broodseinde. Unusually heavy casualties had been inflicted on the enemy and over five thousand prisoners captured; of these the New Zealand Division provided 1,159 drawn from four different Divisions.

Though heavy, the price paid for these successes could not, in view of the results, be regarded as excessive. Moreover the enemy losses had been severe. Indications pointed to a sensible decline in his morale. The coincidence of the two attacks, the enemy losses and the successful British advance, entailed a confusion in his plans and disorganization both among his Infantry and Artillery which ensured quiescence for a few days. His shelling was light and scattered all along the 2nd Army Front, indifferent local counter-attacks, the lack of cohesion no less than the mixture of units for thickening up the line, clearly betrayed his straits.

There are also many references to smashing up counter-attacks and heavy losses inflicted.

I feel I must interpolate here the report of the well-known war correspondent and author, Sir Philip Gibbs, KBE, extracted from his book *From Bapaume to Passchendaele*:—

Broodseinde, 4th October. It has been a bad defeat for them and they do not hide their despair. They did not fight stubbornly for the most part, but ran one way or the other as soon as our barrage passed and revealed our men. Our gunfire had overwhelmed them. In the blockhouses were groups of men who gasped out words of surrender. Here and there they refused to come out till bombs burst inside their steel doors; and here and there they got their machine guns to work and checked our advance for a time on the right of the attack and near Polderhoek, where there has been severe fighting. There was heavy machine gun fire from a fortified farm ruin to the north of Broodseinde, and again from Kron Prinz Farm on the extreme left. The enemy has also put down a heavy machine gun barrage from positions around Passchendaele, but nothing has stopped our men seriously so far.

The New Zealanders and Australians swept up and beyond Gravenstafel and Abraham Heights, went through and past the ruins of Zonnebeke village, and, with great heroism, gained the high ground about Broodseinde, a dominating position giving observation of all the enemy's side of the country. It has been a wonderful battle in the success that surmounted all difficulties, and, if we can keep what we have gained, it will be a victorious achievement.

The weather is bad now, and the rain is heavier with a savage wind blowing, but that is not good for the enemy's plans and may be in our favour now that the day has gone well. Our English troops share the honour of the day with the Anzacs, and all were splendid.

5th October. The men who were fighting in the great battle yesterday, and after the capture of many strong positions, held their ground last night in spite of many German counter-attacks and heavy fire, tell grim tales which all go to build up the general picture of the most slashing defeat we have inflicted on the enemy.

Then follows the story of smashed counter-attacks and a tale of falling morale.

As regards the Germans, our adversary, Ludendorf, comments thus:—

> The battle of the 4th October was extraordinarily severe, and again we only came through it with enormous losses. It was evident that the idea of holding the front line more densely, adopted at my last visit to the front in September, was not the remedy. *Flanders 1917* calls it 'The black day of October 4th.' Opposite the 1st Anzac Corps alone, where the German attack was forestalled, the 45th Reserve Division lost 83 officers and 2,800 other ranks (not including lightly wounded) and the 4th Guard Division 86 officers and 2,700 other ranks. Foot Guard Regiment No. 5 described it as the worst day yet experienced during the war.

German Official Account (XIII, p. 80) sums up:—

> The new battle scheme had not stood the test on the 4th October.

I need only one other quotation out of the many available, and this from General von Kuhl, Prince Ruprecht's Chief of Staff:—

> About the middle of October, the greater part of the Divisions on the rest of the front of the group of Armies had already been engaged in Flanders. On the whole front outside Flanders . . . we had no more than the very minimum of defenders to meet any diversion attacks which might be attempted. The Supreme Command, which hitherto had helped as far as its reserves permitted, was now, in view of the general situation, hardly in a position to provide reinforcements from the other groups of Armies on the Western Front. . . . Crown Prince Ruprecht found himself compelled to consider whether, in the case of his forces proving inadequate, in spite of the many disadvantages involved thereby including the abandonment of the Flanders coast, he should not withdraw the front in Flanders so far back that the Allies would be forced to carry out an entirely new deployment of their Artillery. . . . The loss of ground and the moral disadvantage of retirement would have to be accepted. Preparations were duly made for this operation.

Ruprecht's 1st General Staff Officer records in his diary: 'Quite the heaviest battle to date.'

The Prime Minister visited Haig at G.H.Q. at the end of September and asked him for his views as to the role of the British Army in the event of Russia giving in and to the weakened condition of France and Italy. Haig replied on the

8th October that the effect of Russia's collapse would be to release a number of divisions for the Western Front, but these would be balanced by an influx of divisions from America. The issue must be fought out on the Western Front and it would be waste to send troops to Italy.

> As regards France, neither the French Government nor the Military Authorities will venture to call on their troops for any further great and sustained effort, at any rate before it becomes evident that the enemy's strength has been definitely and finally broken.

Haig concluded by begging (1) that no more frontage should be taken over from the French; (2) that drafts to replace wastage should be trained and sent to France, and (3) that the Cabinet should have 'firm faith in the possibility of final success.' Three conditions which were not vouchsafed to him.

Thus ended the second phase of Passchendaele, culminating in the successful battle of Broodseinde, which was called by our enemy 'The Black Day of October 4th.'

CHAPTER V

Operations in Northern Flanders
Passchendaele, Third Phase—7th October to 13th November

The three successful assaults on the 20th September (Menin Road), the 26th September (Polygon Wood) and the 4th October (Broodseinde) which resulted in the capture of the Gheluvelt Plateau and the ridge about Broodseinde complete the second stage of the Passchendaele operations. The results of these have an important bearing on the remainder of the war and their cumulative effect had left its mark on the German troops which had defended the positions, as was evidenced in their correspondence with their people at home as well as in the opinions of their leaders.

However, the weather then broke, and weather was a fundamental factor more especially in the type of operation recently adopted, that is, an assault on a narrow front in depth, supported by a strong concentration, indeed a great mass of artillery, both field and heavy.

As may be readily imagined, both the massed movement and the massed fire created in wet weather serious destruction of the communications and corresponding difficulties in their repair, especially where the ground consisted of shell holes, mud and water, and there was a constant hostile long-range fire. At each step forward the difficulties were increased by the necessity of moving immense supplies of artillery, ammunition, and of all material required by the troops destined to make the next assault.

As stated by the Official Historian, 'the prospects of the fulfilment of the plan visualized in this programme depended upon the weather.' The plan for the next stage, which was timed to take place on the 9th or 10th of October, involved, in view of

57

the cumulative effect of the three previous successful actions, an effort to increase the intensity and momentum of the assault with the object of penetrating and exploiting any real success; such penetration and exploitation would depend on circumstances at the critical moment. For this purpose it was proposed that preparation should be made for a second attack in the afternoon. But 'the rain which had set in during the afternoon of the 4th October continued in a steady drizzle with occasional heavy showers throughout the next two days and on the 7th came squalls of cold drenching rain.'

The same evening, the 7th October, at a conference at G.H.Q., the two army commanders, Plumer and Gough, told Haig that, though willing to continue, they would welcome a closing down of the campaign. Haig, however, decided to continue the operations with the object of securing the Passchendaele Ridge.

We now enter what I call the third and last phase of the Passchendaele operations which continued for approximately five weeks, and it is these last five weeks which chiefly gave rise to the criticisms and attacks on the reputation of Haig and which, therefore, I want to analyse more particularly.

Perhaps the weightiest reason for reaching this decision was the need to divert German attention from the other allied fronts. The French Army had been granted extra leave, amounting to ten days every four months, which resulted in a permanent reduction of 340,000 in its effective strength, thereby further weakening the French front to that extent. This caused Pétain to make the demand on his British ally to take over an additional front of six divisions in compensation for that loss of effectives. There were also persistent and urgent pleas from Pétain to continue the Flanders operations in order to ensure that the flow of German reserves should be diverted from the French front. Moreover, the French proposed to make a limited attack in Champagne on the 23rd October at Malmaison with selected troops, and it was essential to prevent German reserves moving to that point.

It has since been stated from several sources that Pétain had been successful in restoring, at least to some considerable degree, the spirit and morale of the French Army by this date, and it has been suggested that Haig might well have taken that fact into consideration and have felt justified in relying on the ability of the French to look after their own safety, and thereby release himself from the necessity of providing for their protection from attack. This would be expecting Haig to take the risk of incurring an irreparable catastrophe, a French collapse, in the face of the persistent demands and warnings of the French Commander-in-Chief.

At the actual time in question, mid-October, information was still being regularly received regarding the condition of the French Army; it was confirmed that outwardly, owing to extension of leave periods and other considerable amenities introduced, the superficial aspect had improved, but the atmosphere of defeatism had not diminished at all and there was a distinct disinclination to engage the enemy in any operations, offensive or defensive, and a growing feeling that if anyone had to engage in battle, it should be the British Army. This became even more marked later on. Troops do not recover from the effect of a mutiny in a few weeks, especially of a mutiny of so serious a character and so widespread.

It was not only the condition of the French Army which gave him cause for thought and anxiety. There was also the condition of the Russian Army, the Italian Army, the German Army and the speed of arrival of the Americans. All these factors had their reaction on each other and on the fundamental problems before him. The Russian Army was at this time, mid-October, rapidly disintegrating and disappearing, failing indeed to remain a factor in the war except adversely to release all those German troops which faced it in the East and make an additional thirty to forty divisions available for battle against the British and French in the West. These troops were reputedly not all of the first class but were, nevertheless, active and useful reinforcements for the German Army in the West; some of them were known to be of good quality, well trained and disciplined. They would reach their maximum reinforcement value in the West by the early spring.

But the flower of the German Army was in France and Flanders, and had been very roughly handled in the West in

1916, as well as at Arras, at Messines and particularly in Flanders in 1917. Its casualties had been very heavy; it had been highly trained and was irreplaceable; indeed its losses and exhaustion produced a declension in the efficiency of the Army as a whole. The highly-trained and efficient young officer and non-commissioned officer had ceased to exist. It would take a long time for the German Army in the West to recover its full efficiency and high morale.

Time, therefore, would up to the spring of 1918 give Germany a numerical increase in divisions, but it did not seem likely that in so short a time their morale would recover, for the loss of morale was clearly deep-seated already. Time would benefit the Allies by the increasing arrival of American troops in the summer and autumn of 1918. Time would also benefit the French Army in its effort to recover its morale even partially. But the Germans were well aware of all these factors and must have at an early date reached the obvious conclusion that the earlier they could launch a grand offensive in the West with their maximum force concentrated there, the better would be their chance of success; indeed it offered their only chance, a final grand effort for survival, a final bid for victory. Haig had predicted this as early as August.

Meanwhile, the autumn passed into winter, and this great offensive by Germany on a grand scale became more and more apparent and more certain, and Haig's forecast of the area of attack and the time were not far out.

I must revert for a moment to the conference at G.H.Q. on the 7th October at which Haig disclosed his intention to continue operations to secure the Passchendaele Ridge, in spite of the expression of feeling of Plumer and Gough that they would welcome a closing down of the campaign, and in spite of an evident break in the weather, and I must repeat the request Haig made to the War Cabinet on the following day, the 8th October. He begged:—

(1) That no more frontage should be taken over from the French;
(2) That drafts to replace wastage should be trained and sent to France;
(3) That the Cabinet should have firm faith in the possibility of final success.

These three requests were in conclusion of a letter expressing Haig's views of the situation called for by the Prime Minister at the end of September. All three of them were, of course, vitally important in view of the anticipated German offensive in the spring. It is almost inconceivable to realize that:—

As regards (1) Haig was informed by a letter from Robertson that contrary to his, Haig's, advice the British Government had already approved in principle of the British Army in France taking over more line from the French and that the details were to be arranged between Pétain and himself. This decision had been reached by a conference held at Boulogne on 25th September between the Prime Minister, Robertson and the French authorities, and yet neither the Prime Minister nor Robertson had mentioned the matter to Haig at their subsequent interviews. Haig regarded the decision as a bombshell and, while he was accustomed to such treatment from the Prime Minister, he could not understand it on the part of Robertson.

As regards (2) Haig's urgent request for drafts, it is a matter of common knowledge that the British Army in France was deliberately starved of drafts in the winter of 1917–18.

As regards (3) there was nothing said.

Nevertheless, the Field-Marshal, in spite of everything, was full of faith that he would defeat the German Army in the spring. It is interesting to me to remember that in the spring of 1918 before the German attack, the late Lord Derby told me that Haig was the only man he knew who, in a high and very responsible position, had never failed to express his belief in victory in 1918 and he reminded me of this after victory had been achieved.

Two months after the conference held at G.H.Q. on the 7th October, that is to say on the 7th December, a further army commanders' conference was convened at Doullens. Haig reviewed the position and, after drawing attention to the fact that the next four months would be the critical period of the war, that we had received little or no help from our Allies in the past few months nor could we expect much in the immediate future, he pointed out the Germans would probably be able to assemble thirty additional divisions on the Western Front owing to the defection of Russia. He stressed the urgency of seeing to our defensive organization and issued directions that the defence should be in three zones, 'Forward,' 'Battle' and 'Reserve.' Detailed instructions were issued to all concerned and a warning that all must be prepared to meet a strong hostile offensive in the spring, of which there were already many signs.

Again just one month after the army commanders' conference held at Doullens on 7th December, that is on the 7th January 1918, at a Cabinet Meeting in London, Haig was closely cross-examined on this very subject of the projected German offensive. We know he was convinced that it would take place but, in question and answer at this meeting, he failed to make his views clear. The question was not a fair one and, at the best of times, he was not a skilful dialectician. The question a member of the Cabinet put to him was: 'If you were Ludendorf, would you consider that a smashing offensive would have sufficient chance of success to justify the losses that would be incurred?' It was an impossible question for Haig to answer because it was his genuine opinion that if the Germans attacked in the spring, as it appeared that they would, and if the Allies could withstand their attack, as he believed they could if they received adequate drafts as they should, then the Germans would be defeated not only then, but again in the autumn. He could, however, hardly admit that if he were in command of the German Army he would pursue a policy that would lead to the defeat of that Army in the same year.

He should have replied that he could not answer such a question without knowledge of the condition of morale and numbers of effectives in the German Army in the following spring, nor could he answer without some knowledge of the drafts the British would receive before then. He, however, instead of fencing replied verbally to the effect that: 'If the Germans were wise they would think twice before making the attempt, because if they failed the position would be critical for them.'

There was no suitable answer. In effect, according to Robertson, the Prime Minister seized on the possible interpretation that, if the Germans were wise they would not make the attempt—ergo, there would be no need for the War Office to provide the drafts which he said he so urgently required. Haig attempted to rectify this misinterpretation by submitting a paper the next morning in which he stressed the importance of keeping his divisions up to strength. The Prime Minister tossed the paper on one side and said it was inconsistent with what the Field-Marshal had said verbally. Haig had, in fact, been tricked. But, of course, the Prime Minister knew quite well what was in Haig's mind, and the paper confirmed it.

I think it is possible to summarize what was in the Field-Marshal's mind. I should not have felt able to state it if I had not had the opportunity of talking with him at the time and hearing his views on many of these matters at first hand. Even then I feel that they are impressions left with me—not definite assertions by him.

First, his most important consideration was to keep the French in the war and prevent any substantial attack on their Army, which he believed would be fatal. He was not prepared to take that risk which would be avoided by a continuation of his operations.

Second, he recognized that the weather had broken and would be against him, but there was hope that there might be a bright interlude and the opportunity of dealing another serious blow.

Third, having got most of the way on to the ridge between Ypres and Roulers, he deemed it advisable to get on to the better-drained ground along the top for the benefit of the troops in winter.

Fourth, the Ypres-Roulers watershed is a commanding position and a threat to the enemy as well as a defence to ourselves.

Fifth, we must continue to hold the enemy away from the Malmaison attack which was going to be delivered on the 23rd October by the French.

Sixth, the same as the foregoing, in relation to Lord Byng's projected tank attack at Cambrai for mid-November.

Seventh, the vital but somewhat abstruse problem of morale so important in a predicament such as the present. The assessment of the British, the French and the German morale.

Eighth, the vital question as to what extent his deficiency in manpower in the ranks would be made good.

The seventh and eighth considerations were the imponderables. Given an answer to the eighth it would be possible to assess more accurately the values of the seventh, but both these remained to some extent inconstant though Haig had both evidence and confidence that the British morale would outlast the German.

Ninth, although the submarine menace had lessened in the latter part of the year owing to reducing losses and increase in building, nevertheless the necessity for clearing the Belgian coast of the submarine bases still existed.

Tenth, he had always in his mind the great *Kaiserschlacht* to be delivered in the early spring.

The question of morale was exceedingly important and, indeed, it carried great weight with the Commander-in-Chief. We have studied French morale and we know that it had not recovered, indeed their own leaders pointed out that any strain, offensive or defensive, would probably cause a serious breakdown; and next time it would not be possible to recover.

German morale was of a different type. Their field discipline was tougher and more durable than that of the French, who were more mercurial, more temperamental and excitable. Given an equal strain one would expect the German soldier to continue fighting stubbornly after the Frenchman gave in. The Germans had, after all their heavy fighting since the beginning of the war on both fronts, and more especially during the battles of Verdun and the Somme in 1916, Arras, the Aisne, Messines and above all Flanders in 1917, been severely tried. Already in July 1917 reports of falling morale, both among the civil population and the German Army, were rife, the seeds of weariness and discontent were existent. But by the middle of October there was a steady flow of evidence of 'diminishing morale,' 'shattered in spirit and in reserves,' 'broken divisions,' '88 German divisions had been engaged in the Flanders battles alone, 22 of them twice.' The effects of the recent battles were correctly gauged at the time by British Intelligence and they were fully confirmed by all authorities concerned, by Prince Ruprecht, by his Chief of Staff, Von Kuhl, by the German Official Monograph on the battle of Flanders, and by the German official account. On the 11th October Prince Ruprecht was considering withdrawal to save men and material. It was the Flanders offensive, or rather the triple victory of Broodseinde, which turned the signs of war-weariness and discontent into definite evidence of despondency and loss of morale. Haig was subsequently abundantly proved to have been right about the deterioration in German morale. The German official explanation of the '*disaster*' of the 4th October (battle of Broodseinde) is that divisions were no longer what they had been as a result of nervous exhaustion, fatigue and bloody losses, and so the tale goes on in a similar vein.

As regards the British troops, Haig's view was that in spite of the severe casualties sustained and the serious and prolonged strain, both mental and physical, the British troops would have a greater staying power. The German people as well as the troops were beginning to suspect that they were fighting a losing battle, and there was much feeling that they would be wise to make peace if such could be made on reasonable terms. This was not the case with the British troops; they were tired out and longing for peace, but they had no doubts as to the result. The Dominion troops, Anzacs and Canadians, fought on as well as they had ever done and that was up to a very high standard. Haig, I think, judged that physical conditions of ground and weather were no better on the German side than on ours and, indeed, the German official opinion was that they were much worse.

The serious effect of the prolonged war, on a total basis, and of the character of the warfare, was that of the abnormal volume of casualties which it produced. This drain on the manhood of the nation fell heavily and inevitably on the natural leaders and on those who could least well be spared for the future welfare of the country. This was inevitable, but it weighed heavily on the mind of the Commander-in-Chief.

There were responsible but misinformed people who stated that both Foch and Pétain were against the Flanders offensive and its continuance. Quite the contrary was the case. Foch, as Chief of the Staff, expressed the view that 'the British must continue the battle in Flanders which is indispensable in order to tie down the enemy and prevent him from sending reinforcements to Italy'—and, further, considered that 'the Flanders campaign was indispensable to the right conduct of the war.'

As regards Pétain, he begged for the Flanders operations to be continued, and volunteered to co-operate with the French 1st Army of six divisions. The French official account actually states that, when General Anthoine visited Haig he brought with him the message from Pétain: 'L'offensive des Flandres doit être assurée d'un succes absolu, *impérieusement exigé par les facteurs moraux du moment.*' (Italicized in original.) It seems fairly clear that at this time the French Generals held the view very strongly that we, the British Army, should protect the French Army by continuing our offensive in Flanders, that we should take over more of the front line from the French in order that they should have longer leave, that we should go to the assistance of the Italians by sending them heavy artillery and five British divisions, and that we should continue to fight single-handed notwithstanding that the full weight of the German assault would in all probability fall on the British in the following spring.

It is of interest to note the report of a conversation between Repington, who was at that time military correspondent of *The Times*, and Plumer, as recorded by the latter's Chief Staff Officer, Harrington, and quoted by Duff Cooper in his book on Haig, Vol. II, page 166. Repington visited Plumer's army in October 1917 and

> found Plumer heart and soul for the Flanders offensive. I asked him whether he was thinking of his present tactical objectives or whether he had in mind the strategy of the next year 1918 and its possibilities. He, Plumer, said he had both and had fully considered the future possibilities.

This disposes of the rumour that Plumer was not in accord with Haig.

Since Haig made his decision on the 7th October to continue the Flanders offensive and secure the ridge up to the village of Passchendaele, although convinced he was taking the right course, he must have felt as the weeks passed by that his anxieties regarding the strength and reinforcement of his armies were by no means being allayed. Indeed his anxiety must have been increased not only by failure to send out the required drafts but by the dissipation of his available force through the necessity to meet the demands for assistance on the part of his Allies.

He obviously banked on being supported from home to help him to face the trial of strength which was looming ahead.

So Haig decided to carry on having in mind the probable course of events next year and after the most careful consideration of all the factors which I have already discussed. This last phase continued until the 13th November, our troops having by then reached and secured a good part of the Passchendaele Ridge, including the village of that name. To get a proper perspective of this period, which was the most seriously criticized and which was carried out under great hardship and the most trying physical conditions, one must realize that the total numbers of infantry engaged during these five weeks was actually no greater than those engaged during the one day, the 31st July.

Slight progress was made on the 9th and 12th and then he decided to pause and await some improvement in the weather. At a conference at Cassel on the 13th October with army commanders, Haig stressed the importance of securing the main ridge and engaging the enemy's attention to assist indirectly the French attack which was due to be delivered at Malmaison on the 23rd October, and Byng's attack with tanks facing Cambrai about mid-November. An attack was delivered on the 26th October and again on the 30th October, chiefly by the Canadian Corps which had been moved to the battle area. The Canadians by the 13th November had been responsible for the capture and retention of the Passchendaele high ground. This result reflects the high standard of efficiency of the Canadian Corps and its four divisions. I quote from the

Official History:

> Once again, as at Vimy Ridge and on Hill 70 earlier in the year, the tenacity and endurance of Canada's splendid contribution to the British Imperial Forces were manifest.

The French carried out their successful operation at Malmaison on the 23rd October, which gave them great satisfaction and encouragement.

As to the battle of Cambrai, which took place on the 20th November, and the German counter-attack which was delivered on the 30th, I do not propose to enter into details. Until the five British divisions had been ordered to Italy, and a further four earmarked from the Fourth Army to relieve the French by taking over an additional sector of the front, I feel that the operation would have been fully justified and desirable, but, so late in the year and with the reduction and indeed absence of reserve power, it is doubtful. There was, in fact, insufficient reserve power either to exploit success or to meet a powerful counter-attack, and the action involved a considerable risk especially in view of the future strain which he saw in the not far distant future.

Haig, however, pursued the course he had chosen. The attack by a large number of tanks was admirably executed and successful, but the heavy counter-attack delivered subsequently by the Germans largely neutralized the results and the battle petered out.

This Cambrai operation and the employment of tanks cannot, however, in principle be disposed of in a few words; an operation of this type must be considered in relation to the campaign of 1917 as a whole.

There have been and still are criticisms from intelligent and responsible sources as to (*a*) why Flanders was chosen as the area of operations for the second half of 1917, and (*b*) why the Flanders operations were not stopped after the first setback in August and when the submarine menace began to subside, or even when the weather broke in October, and (*c*) why the Cambrai operation with tanks was not adopted earlier and on a wider scale.

I had many talks with the Commander-in-Chief on this topic

The Author - Major General Sir John Davidson KCMG CB DSO. In 1915 he became Operations Officer, First Army, before being made Haig's Director of Operations after the latter became Commander-in-Chief of the BEF in place of Field Marshal Sir John French in December of that year. His unique position makes his account particularly valuable and, as the last surviving member of Haig's inner circle, he believed that he had a vital story to tell.

Douglas Haig at the age of 23, after he had joined the 7th (Queen's Own) Hussars in February 1885.

Field Marshal Sir John French (*left*) with Generals Joffre and Haig at the front in 1915. Relations between French and Haig, never cordial, further deteriorated when the former was replaced by the latter that December.

Haig accompanies Edward, Prince of Wales on a visit to the Front.

Haig (who spoke French well) and Clemenceau meeting a cleric (unknown). Haig and Clemenceau struck up a strong friendship despite the political and military pressures.

Field Marshal Sir Douglas Haig, leaving the 3rd Canadian divisional headquarters, February 1918.

Haig watches as Maréchal Joffre congratulates (temporary) Major General RHK Butler on his appointment as Deputy Chief of the General Staff.

French troops toil in atrocious conditions, seen here rescuing mules from a shell hole. The collapse of French morale in 1917 and ensuing mutinies were a constant concern to Haig and the British High Command.

URGENT OPERATIONS PRIORITY to

    4th Cav. Bde.
    3rd Div.
    Guards Div.
    62nd Div.
    12th Sqdn. RAF
    Corps H.A.   R.A.

Guards Div.	12th Sqdn RAF	A.A.A.C.	A.D.A.S.
2nd Div.	4th Corps	R.A.	A.P.M.
3rd Div.	Adv. 17th Corps	Q	G.I.
62nd Div.	3rd Army	C.E.	Diary
Corps H.A.	Corps Cyclists	D.D.M.S.	5th Corps
4th Cav.Bde.			

G. 281   11

Hostilities will cease at 11.00 hrs. today 11th Nov. AAA Troops
will stand fast on line reached at that hour which will be
reported by wire to Corps H.Q. AAA Defensive precautions
will be maintained AAA There is to be no intercourse of any
description with the enemy AAA No Germans are to be allowed
to enter our lines any doing so will be taken prisoner AAA
All moves of 3rd Div. for Nov.11 are cancelled AAA 4th Cav.
Bde. will carry out its moves to BOUSSOIS AAA ACKNOWLEDGE AAA
Addsd 4th Cav. Bde. 3rd Div. Gds. Div. 62nd Div. 12th Sqdn
RAF rptd remainder List B.
H.A., R.A.
                (today)

Adv. 6th Corps.
        hrs.
                                              BGGS

The historic Armistice telegram received at GHQ on 11 November 1918.
Major JH Drake OBE MC TD, realising the significance of the moment, had
the message signed by key members of Haig's staff, including the C-in-C
himself. (Reproduced with kind permission of Major Drake's grandson, Michael Stewart, Esq.)

A group of German POWs guarded by a Tommy post the Armistice.

Field Marshal Sir Douglas Haig leading the British Empire troops in the Paris Victory Parade, March 1919.

Field Marshal The Earl Haig in full ceremonial dress. He died suddenly in London on 30 January 1928. His reputation suffered after his death and opinion remains divided as to his ability. The Author, like so many of his contemporaries of all ranks, held him in the highest esteem.

after the war; he held strong views on this subject and I will try to express them here. Having seized the initiative he was determined to hold it; he recognized that he must keep the French in the war, that he must wear down the Germans physically and morally, and he recognized further that he could only achieve these two objects by attacking the enemy on a battleground which must be defended yard by yard. He was impressed by the statement made by Jellicoe in June 1917, 'If the Army cannot get the Belgian ports, the Navy cannot hold the Channel and the war is as good as lost.' On the 21st July the War Cabinet gave 'formal approval of the Commander-in-Chief's plan and promised full support.' He believed that with reasonable weather and fortune he could gain the Belgian ports. In effect he encountered both bad weather in August and misfortune in the late arrival of the French contingent.

Many other alternatives had been considered at home, the most popular being to remain on the defensive in France, and attempt to knock out Austria or Turkey. Fortunately Haig would have none of these for they would have involved losing the initiative which might well have resulted in the destruction of the French Army and loss of the war.

Haig persisted in the Flanders operation, and there appeared to be still a chance of securing the German submarine bases, but in late August and early September the importance of securing these bases diminished while the chance of doing so also appeared to be less.

During September the battle might have been moved, but the process would have been lengthy and the retention of German troops in front of the British would have been doubtful; the preparations for the renewed assault on the Flanders Ridge were under way and due to begin on 20th September. These operations were useful and successful and continued until 4th October, when the weather broke.

Byng, commanding the 3rd Army, came to G.H.Q. on the 16th September with a plan for the Cambrai operation with tanks; this appealed to Haig (who had kept the closest watch on design and production of tanks, and their handling in the field) and instructions were issued to work out details, troops and armour required and available, and dates. Tanks were withdrawn from Flanders. A conference was called by the 3rd Army on the 26th October to settle final details, but on this very date Haig was called upon to send two divisions to Italy, to be followed by two more, and probably a further two to stem the Caporetto catastrophe. The training of infantry with tanks was proceeding.

I believe that steps would have been taken to move the field of operations to the 3rd Army front much earlier, with the object of opening a new offensive and making use of tanks, but for two reasons: firstly, September was a dry month in Flanders, and secondly the three battles on 20th and 26th September and 4th October were highly successful and seemed to have opened up considerable possibilities; Haig was anxious to exploit the favourable outlook and continued the battle. But the weather broke on 7th October.

With the knowledge we possessed in November of the almost inevitable trial of strength which would take place in the spring when the Germans would have brought over the heavy reinforcement of divisions released from the Russian Front, and before the arrival of the Americans, I believe our wisest course would have been to cancel the Cambrai operations, conserve the tank force, and settle down to the necessary and urgent measures to meet the German onslaught.

By the middle of November it was very improbable that the Germans would undertake any offensive action before the early spring.

With the end of the Flanders offensive and the Cambrai battle, the stage was getting set for 1918.

It is possible to arrive at some conclusion as to whether the Flanders operations did contribute to the victory achieved the following year, apart from their necessity for the purpose of protecting the French against attack. It is true that the British casualties during this period, 31st July to the 10th November, were actually 238,000 total battle and trench wastage; these are, as stated, contemporary figures and no effort to gerrymander them. The casualty figures quoted by Lloyd George and some others at 400,000 were definitely incorrect and exaggerated.

Von Kuhl depicts the state of the German Army after the Flanders battle thus:—

> The supply of reinforcements was bound to become more difficult in the ensuing years, so that in the end the conduct of the war was definitely influenced by it. On this point Field-Marshal Haig has been quite right; if he did not actually break through the German front, *the Flanders battle consumed the German strength to such a degree that the harm done could no longer be repaired. The sharp edge of the German sword had become jagged.*

And here is a German extract:—

> A hundred thousand leave-men told the German Home Front by word of mouth the ever-growing superiority of the enemy, particularly in weapons of destruction.

The German official account relates:—

> Divisions disappeared by dozens into the turmoil of the battle, only to emerge from the witches' cauldron after a short period, thinned and exhausted, often reduced to a miserable remnant. Significant signs of strain manifested themselves.

Crown Prince Ruprecht states in his diary:—

> Most perturbing is the fact that our troops are steadily deteriorating.

The British Historian states:—

> The Germans were, it is now known, beaten and Crown Prince Ruprecht was making preparations for a withdrawal.

German official judgement of the Flanders offensive seems to be fairly conclusive. The long view taken by Haig is deemed to have been the right view. It confirms the deterioration of the German morale and the damage inflicted on the German Army. I must offer here three further short quotations:

Flanders 1917, it is stated that:—

> In the year 1918 it turned out that their success (in Flanders) definitely contributed to the result that the war ended in favour of the Allies.

Von Kuhl, *Der Weltkrieg 1914–18 Band II:*—

> There can be no doubt remaining that English tenacity in fact bridged over the crisis in France. . . . The sacrifice that England has made in the cause of the Entente was justified by the result.

The German Official History sums up:—

Above all, the battle had led to an excessive expenditure of German Forces. The casualties were so great that they could no longer be covered, and the already reduced battle strength of battalions sank significantly lower.

The best proof, however, lies in the final result. The Germans made two great assaults on the British Army the next year, 1918, with an overwhelming numerical superiority, on the 21st March and 9th April; the first was held and collapsed within 12 days, and the second within three weeks. German morale failed to last the course.

Ludendorf has referred, on two occasions during the war, to a 'Black Day.' The *first* '*Black Day*' was 4th October 1917, the battle of Broodseinde, when the German morale showed signs of distinct deterioration, and the tide had begun very obviously and definitely to turn. The *second* '*Black Day*' was 8th August 1918, the battle of Amiens, when the German morale had cracked and the tide was running in full spate towards victory.

This is the last of the three chapters dealing with the series of battles fought on the ridge between Ypres and Roulers, spread over three and a half months, and commonly known as Passchendaele, and on this period I should like briefly to summarize a few final remarks.

Being wise after the event, and notwithstanding the results achieved on the first day, I think it may be accepted that the objective of the opening battle on the 31st July should have been confined to wearing down or attrition; the situation was not ripe for penetration or exploitation at that stage; but who was to know that the Germans would not give way then in fine weather, as they did two months later in wet weather. The Australian Official Historian remarks: 'It by no means follows that Haig was wrong, but in the mixture of motives lay grave disadvantages.'

Haig and his two army commanders were in full agreement on the course to be pursued, but the result of the effort to push out too far on the first day was that the battlefront became ragged, and in that condition further progress became difficult.

I agree with Gough that it would have been better if Plumer, who had been in front of the enemy's position for two years, and knew the importance of the key position of Gheluvelt Plateau and the country round about, had been placed in command of the major operation from the outset, and charged with the capture of that position, while Gough took a secondary part in the North.

Haig recognized that the operations were not progressing on satisfactory lines, for the reasons above stated. From the moment he decided to make the change, he did so with rapidity and precision both in regard to the tactics and aim of the battle as had been previously recommended, as well as in the command, with results which are fully described in Chapter IV dealing in particular with the three battles of Menin Road, Polygon Wood and Broodseinde.

I have already recited the four official reports of the four official historians, representing the four respective countries— Great Britain, Australia, New Zealand and Germany—which took part in those three battles.

I have no shadow of doubt that the cumulative effect of the Flanders offensive as a whole and those three battles in particular damaged German morale and staying power so that, in spite of the overwhelming numerical superiority and initial success, the great *Kaiserschlacht* of the spring of 1918 petered out and failed completely, leading to defeat and surrender four months later. This is confirmed by the Germans as stated in Chapter IX.

In spite of the heavy casualties and hardships experienced during 1917, the morale of the British and Commonwealth troops throughout 1918 remained remarkably high.

CHAPTER VI

Organization and Preparation to meet German Offensive, 1918

W̲ᴇ have seen in the previous chapter that with the conclusion of the battle of Cambrai, all active operations ceased for the winter. Haig held a conference of army commanders on 7th December 1917 to review the situation and drew attention to the forthcoming German assault in the spring which would be reinforced by divisions released from the Eastern Front, and stressed the urgency of seeing to our defensive organization. He issued directions that the defence should be arranged in three zones—forward zone, battle zone and reserve zone. Detailed instructions were issued to all concerned.

Meanwhile the question of the extent of the respective fronts held by the British and French armies was raised by our allies urgently, and, as already stated, it was agreed at an Anglo-French Conference held at Boulogne on the 25th September, without the knowledge of Haig, to accept the principle of the extension of the British front; the limit of extension and the time it should take place was to be left for arrangement between the two Commanders-in-Chief. Haig wrote to the War Office on the 16th October objecting to any decision on the extension of his front at any allied conference at which he was not present. But the matter had gone too far.

Clemenceau and Foch were particularly insistent that the British should take over as far as Berry-au-Bac, which seemed excessive, and Pétain also was rather sceptical as to the possibility of so great an extension, and pressed instead for a six-division front taking up as far as Barisis, just south of the River Oise.

Meanwhile the Italian collapse at Caporetto and retreat in disorder to the River Piave, with the loss of a quarter of a million prisoners and large numbers of guns, created consternation in Paris and London. Robertson and Foch, followed by the British Prime Minister and representatives of the French Government, hurried to the Italian front to see what could be done to restore the situation.

Now Lord French, after he had ceased to command the British Army in France, and General Sir Henry Wilson, who had ceased to command the 4th Corps in France and ceased to be head of the British Mission at French Headquarters, both having spare time, were invited by the War Cabinet to study the whole wide question of the conduct and control of operations, not only of the British but of the allied forces in every theatre, and to report thereon. Accordingly Wilson had written a paper making certain recommendations such as the formation of an Inter-Allied War Council to secure unity and ensure co-ordination and co-operation of the allied plans.

The leaders of Britain and France on arrival in Italy decided to send several British and French divisions to reinforce the Italian Army at once and this was done, and incidentally delayed the take over of additional front of the French Army in France by the British.

A conference of these leaders, including the Italian Government, was then held on the 7th November at Rapallo, when the following decisions were reached:—

1. To establish and organize a Supreme War Council with a Permanent Military Representative from each Power, as well as the Prime Minister and a Minister from each of the Great Powers whose armies are engaged in fighting on that particular front.

2. The Supreme War Council oversees the conduct of the war, prepares recommendations and watches the execution of such recommendations and makes reports.

3. The commanders and general staffs of the armies remain responsible to their respective governments.

4. All war plans to be submitted to the Supreme War Council, which contains one Permanent Military Representative from each Power to act as technical adviser. This representative to be kept posted by his own govern-

ment on all proposals, information and documents regarding the conduct of the war. The situation and disposable means are to be watched day by day.

5. The Supreme War Council is to be located normally at Versailles, and it is intended to function once a month. It can, however, be located anywhere else according to circumstances and meet as required.

6. The Permanent Military Representatives were: France—General Foch; Britain—General Wilson; Italy—General Cadorna.

The Council met at once, and among the many matters discussed was the question of the respective fronts to be held by the British and French Armies, but no decision was reached in spite of a great deal of discussion. The Supreme War Council then met on 30th January and the session lasted till the 2nd February. The Council had placed on record a resolution in the shape of a compromise that the British front should be extended as far as the River Ailette, and Haig had immediately dispatched a letter to the War Cabinet protesting against any further extension beyond Barisis and requesting that he might be relieved of his command if his recommendation was disregarded. All concerned at the Supreme War Council submitted papers showing arguments every way, and, in short, Haig and Pétain settled the matter by agreeing on Barisis as the dividing line. This in fact was still responsible for overstretching the British line to 130 miles with Belgian troops on the left and Portuguese on the left centre. We had fifty-seven divisions, of which forty-seven would be reduced from twelve to nine battalions—and there would be inadequate reinforcements provided to support these. Haig further expressed the view that in the coming assault of the whole German Army we must be prepared for 100,000 casualties a month.

Having disposed of the question of extension of the British front, the Council then dealt with two other important items on the agenda:

1. Manpower, and
2. Unity of control.

As regards (1) (Manpower), reinforcements and drafts were

76

required in France; it was there that the main issue was about to be contested. It was essential, and indeed vital, that steps should have been taken in the autumn of 1917 to provide the necessary strength, by an extension of the military age, if necessary, as well as by a radical reduction of our commitments in the secondary theatres of war. Haig, as we have already seen, had stressed the urgent necessity at the beginning of October of concentrating in the main theatre of war where the decision would be reached, he had persistently opposed the equally persistent proposal to transfer allied offensive power to Italy with the intention of attacking the Austrians, and he had demanded reinforcements and drafts to be sent to France in time to be trained before the storm broke. He was not alone in urging such measures, and commanders of the Allies in Paris had already done likewise.

In spite of all Haig's efforts and warnings, it was not until January 1918 that steps were taken to provide an additional 100,000 men; none of these arrived in time to be trained for the battle, and in any case the numbers were quite inadequate. There were more than enough trained men available in the United Kingdom, none under nineteen, to fill up the ranks of the infantry to establishment, but these were retained at home. No steps were taken in time to bring over to France the requisite troops which might have been made available from other theatres of war. The effect of this manpower starvation was that at the eleventh hour the numbers in battalions and brigades were cut down and the normal organization of units and formations altered, and this naturally did not conduce to accustomed tactical arrangement and efficiency in the field. To sum up, the question of manpower and shortage of reinforcements had been neglected by the Government; if it had not been for the morale and splendid spirit of the British and Commonwealth troops there might well have been a catastrophe.

As regards (2) (Unity of control), this subject had already been under discussion between G.H.Q., the War Office and the War Cabinet. There were three alternatives:—

(a) The appointment of a Generalissimo,
(b) The establishment of an executive War Board of the

77

Supreme War Council with Foch as chairman, whose special duty would be the formation and manipulation of a general reserve,

(c) The exercise of control by collaboration between the two chiefs (French and British) or their representatives.

(a) *The Appointment of a Generalissimo.* No doubt this alternative would have been the choice of the military and it would have been Haig's choice, if it had not been for the location of responsibility for the safety of an army serving under the command of a foreign Generalissimo, which created a serious difficulty. For example, take the case of the British Army serving under a French Generalissimo; the latter could not accept responsibility for the safety of the British Army; if the French Generalissimo issued a hazardous order to the British, the British Commander obviously could not bear the responsibility; the British War Cabinet would hardly be likely to accept the responsibility. In whom then could the responsibility reside? It was from a military point of view of such paramount importance to appoint a Generalissimo that this solution could not be finally thrown out. Yet it was thrown out at the time, and the Prime Minister gave his reason in the House of Commons on the 19th November 1917 as follows (*Hansard*):—

Having agreed that it is desirable to get some sort of central authority in order to co-ordinate—I use the word my Right Honourable Friend used, there is no better. What is the best method of doing it? He examined three alternatives. I am in complete agreement with him in his views with regard to the first two. The first has been put forward in very responsible quarters, and that is the appointment of a generalissimo of the whole of the Forces of the allies. I agree with him. Personally I am utterly opposed to that suggestion for reasons which it would not be desirable to enter into. It would not work. It would produce real friction, and might really produce not merely friction between the Armies, but friction between the Nations and the Governments.

The reasons to which the Prime Minister referred were, of course, the difficulties and dangers regarding the impact of responsibility which I have mentioned above.

French military opinion on the subject was much the same as our own, and both are very well depicted as follows. When discussing the subject of unity of command with a senior French general and he was saying how important it was to appoint a

Generalissimo in spite of the difficulties, he added, 'Never fear, we must have one, but we shall have to wait until "*après la prochaine tape*".' He was quite right, for when the crisis arose on the 26th March 1918, the greater fear of a catastrophe drove the British Government to accept the Generalissimo; it however shortly after imposed certain safeguards which in effect threw the responsibility back to the British Commander-in-Chief, but that was inevitable. Two cases of battledore and shuttlecock of responsibility which arose will be described later, and I shall refer to them as the Smuts and Wilson cases.

As regards the other two alternatives an effort was made to establish the Executive War Board (of the supreme War Council) and regulations were drafted for the formation, movement, location and general manipulation of a general reserve. Haig stated that he would do his best to work in complete harmony with the Executive War Board, but that, at the present moment, owing to the extended front held by the British armies and the lack of reinforcements, he was unwilling to allocate any of his own divisions to the inter-allied reserve. In fact, the actual reserves which he held were not adequate for the support of the British front alone under the existing military situation. Meanwhile little or no advance was made in the formation of a general reserve, since none of the Commanders-in-Chief felt himself strong enough to allocate any of his reserve troops for any purpose outside his own command. The Executive War Board without a general reserve could obviously not function, and it therefore fell into abeyance.

Action had, however, been taken by Haig and Pétain to *collaborate and co-ordinate* the arrangements regarding the location and use of their respective reserves in the event of the enemy delivering an offensive against either or both armies. Shortly, these arrangements consisted of detailed plans for the concentration of French reserves in certain areas behind the British front, and of British troops in certain areas behind the French front. Special attention was paid to the case which actually arose, namely, a heavy hostile attack about the point of junction of the two armies, and arrangements were made for the rapid movement of eight divisions by rail, road and bus to the neighbourhood of the line Noyon–Lassigny, to be followed, if necessary, by a subsequent and similar concentration of troops in the neighbourhood of Amiens. We shall see later how this broke down.

Incidentally, after the session of the Supreme War Council, that is on 4th February, the Army Council submitted a formal protest to the effect that if an Executive Board such as that proposed were formed and its duties assigned as stated, it would deprive the Army Council of its responsibilities, and violate the trust imposed on it, under the Constitution. In view of this, the office of Permanent British Representative of the Supreme War Council was created and its duties assigned. This involved the replacement of Robertson by Wilson, and the reversion to the old practice in force prior to 1915. This, from the point of view of the Army, was not a change for the better, and the loss of Robertson particularly was considered by the Army to be serious.

It had been agreed that the plan of operations was simply that the British and French should hold their respective fronts and await the arrival of sufficient American troops to enable the Allies to take the offensive.

The relief of the French troops as far south as Barisis was completed by the 30th January, thus extending the British to cover a front of 130 miles, being the most important and difficult sector of the whole Allied front. Moreover, as foreshadowed, British divisions (except Dominion divisions) were reduced from a twelve-battalion to a nine-battalion basis during the month of February. Haig's urgent request to the War Cabinet four months earlier, that he should not be called on to take over more front from the French, and that drafts and reinforcements should be sent to him early to train for the battle, had not only elicited no response, but the establishments of the bulk of his divisions was reduced by twenty-five per cent. The time of the great German assault was approaching.

By the middle of February 1918 it became evident that the enemy was assembling his mighty army of over 190 divisions on the principle of concentration on the decisive front, and there were definite indications that the attack would take place at an early date. Constant air-reconnaissances showed by the work on communications, road and rail, and on ammunition dumps that the attack would fall roughly on the 3rd and 5th Army fronts, although there were indications of preparation farther north into Flanders. Towards the end of February and subsequently it became more and more certain that the attack would take place on the sector previously indicated.

A diagram of the distribution of the British armies as on the morning of 21st March 1918 is shown herein, and it is to be noted that at least sixty-four divisions of the German Army took part in the operations of the first day of the battle, a number considerably in excess of the total forces composing the entire British Army in France. The majority of these divisions had been specially trained for offensive operations.

The whole assault of these sixty-four divisions fell on the 3rd and 5th Armies, which, as will be seen in the diagram, disposed of only twenty-six divisions and three cavalry divisions, with four divisions in G.H.Q. Reserve. The brunt of the assault was met by the 5th Army, which was holding a front of no less than forty-two miles in quite inadequate strength, and which had only taken over the front from the French a few weeks before.

The condition of the defences taken over so recently was deplorable and necessitated the troops being occupied with getting them into some sort of shape, instead of undergoing training which was so urgent.

The 5th Army was numerically overwhelmed and fell back fighting stubbornly over ground which could be given up under pressure in this area without serious consequence. Nevertheless there were very anxious times during a period of fourteen days, after which the enemy was finally halted and held. The promised French support on its right flank failed and Pétain was superseded.

These operations have been described as a disaster; they were nothing of the sort; they constituted a part of the prelude to final victory. The course of the battle is briefly described in the following chapter.

GERMAN OFFENSIVE 21st MARCH 1918

DISTRIBUTION OF BRITISH TROOPS

(Belgian and French troops Dixmude to sea coast)		Divs. in Reserve	Heavy Guns	Divs. in Fnt. Line	Army Frontage
A NORTHERN Channel Ports: Dunkirk, Calais, Boulogne Maintenance of sufficient troops in area essential. No ground could be yielded in this area.	2nd Army (Plumer) Ypres	3 divs. [2 divs. in G.H.Q. Reserve]	388	9 divs.	23 miles
B In the CENTRAL portion lie the collieries of France and important tactical features and lateral communications. Little if any ground could be yielded except in Lys Valley.	1st Army Arment-ières La Bassée Lens	4 divs. [2 divs. in G.H.Q. Reserve]	276	10 divs. plus 2 Portuguese divs.	33 miles
C SOUTHERN Area S.E. of Arras. Ground could be given up under pressure without serious consequences. Forward area consists chiefly of wide expanse of ground devastated in enemy's withdrawal in previous spring. This is area indicated for German attack—object—separation of British and French armies—capture of important centre of	3rd Army (Byng) Arras	4 divs. [2 divs. in G.H.Q. Reserve]	461	10 divs.	28 miles
Amiens. Rather more than half of British force allocated to defence of this sector, also arrangements previously made for rapid reinforcement by road, rail and bus of this area from British in the north and from the French in south.	Amiens Somme	1 div. Distance from front line to Amiens approximately 40 miles	515	11 divs.	42 miles
	5th Army (Gough) St. Quentin	3 cavalry divs. [2 divs. in G.H.Q. Reserve]			

Barisis (Junction with French 6th Army)

The French front linked up with the British 5th Army (see diagram) on the south at Barisis. There were two factors which influenced Pétain in the disposition of his reserves. Firstly, there was the possibility of attack through Switzerland and via Belfort, and it had always been present in the minds of the French. Secondly, there were indications both from preparations being observed and information being received that attacks might be launched on Rheims and the Chemin des Dames on the Aisne front.

This latter fact influenced Pétain not only in the initial distribution of his reserves, but also, and what is more important, it continued to influence him after the battle had opened, in holding back his troops and preventing a whole-hearted support of the British.

As the days of March passed by, the situation became clear beyond doubt; not only the front to be attacked could be accurately defined, but the date could almost be fixed within a few days. On the 20th I motored out to visit the 4th and 6th Corps and examine some aerial photographs, and stayed for the night with Byng at 3rd Army Headquarters. At 5 a.m. on the following morning the battle opened with the artillery bombardment, and a heavy mist.

CHAPTER VII

The German Offensives of 21st March and 9th April 1918

This chapter is an extract from a document entitled *Operations on the Western Front 1916–18* (pages 58 to 66) and deals with the great offensives launched by the German Army on the 21st March and 9th April 1918 against the British front, known in Germany as the KAISERSCHLACHT.

The document was drawn up by the General Staff at G.H.Q., revised by the Chief of the General Staff, and subsequently approved by the Field-Marshal Commanding-in-Chief.

The German Army was defeated and their offensive brought to a standstill by the British Army, after some five weeks of severe fighting. The reason given by the Germans for their defeat is stated in Chapter IX.

THE German offensive began on 21st March and its course is fully described in Sir Douglas Haig's dispatch of 6th August 1918.

The British front was driven in from its right to opposite Cambrai. Our troops were falling back with the loss of many prisoners and guns. The situation, especially on the British right, had by the evening of the 22nd become extremely critical. The enemy was reported to have broken through and there were inadequate reserves with which to oppose him.

On the 23rd March at about 4 p.m. Sir Douglas Haig and the Chief of the General Staff met General Pétain at Dury. The situation was discussed, and General Pétain explained what he could do to assist the right of the British 5th Army in accordance with the arrangements made during the early part of the year. The 5th Army would hold the line of the Somme as long as possible or until the arrival of General Pelle with six French divisions at Guisgard. On about the 30th six more divisions would begin to arrive at Montdidier and would be commanded by General Humbert. Both Humbert's and Pelle's forces would be under General Fayolles. The concentration would be slow as the majority of the troops were coming from Alsace.

General Pétain was very anxious regarding the Rheims front, where he expected to be attacked about the 26th March, and was unwilling to move his reserves from that neighbourhood, which was obviously the locality from which to draw reinforcements if they were to reach the British front in time.

On the 24th the Chief of the General Staff met General Fayolles at Villers Bretonneux. The line of the Somme had been forced by the enemy at certain points and the 5th Army was falling back fighting hard. Very little assistance was being given by the French divisions on our right who were falling back but were not being seriously attacked. Fayolles said he would have no new troops available till the 28th, but was willing to order a counter-attack with the French troops on the spot in conjunction with the 5th Army to restore the situation south of Peronne where so far the enemy had only got a foothold on the west bank of the Somme. In order to facilitate matters, the Chief of the General Staff agreed to place all British troops south and west of the Somme under General Fayolles. Orders for the counter-attack on the morning of the 25th were issued, but the attack never materialized as the French troops did not turn up. It appeared that the bulk of the French troops were arriving by bus without their guns and only 50 rounds of S.A.A.; consequently their commanders would not throw them into the fight but marched away on the approach of the enemy.

At 8 p.m. on the 24th, the Chief of the General Staff met Sir Douglas Haig at 3rd Army Headquarters at Beauquesne, and after explaining the situation, left with the Commander-in-Chief to meet General Pétain at Dury at 11 p.m. General Pétain was much disturbed at the condition of affairs, but was convinced that the main German attack had still to be delivered and that it would be made in great strength on the French front in Champagne. He would do what he could to keep touch with the British armies west of Amiens, but in case of the enemy continuing to press his attacks on Amiens he had issued orders for the French divisions concentrating about Montdidier to fall

85

back south-west and cover Paris. This closed the meeting, and on arrival at headquarters at Beaurépaire, * Sir Douglas Haig wired to the Chief of the Imperial General Staff to come to France in order that the Commander-in-Chief for the whole front might be appointed as soon as possible.

The situation on Sunday, the 24th, was extremely critical. It looked as though the French were not going to fight but withdraw to cover Paris. The two allies must, therefore, if the enemy continued his offensive in the present direction, become separated, and if Amiens junction fell into the hands of the Germans a most critical situation would be created.

On the 25th Sir Douglas Haig handed a note to General Weygand to give to M. Clemenceau and General Foch, pointing out the obvious intention of the enemy to force the British and French armies apart. This must be prevented at all costs and the French must come to a definite decision and concentrate a sufficient force, at least twenty divisions, astride the Somme west of Amiens. There could be no danger now of any attack in force on the Champagne front in view of the number of German divisions concentrated or engaged on the British front.

On the same date, i.e. the 25th, Lord Milner and the C.I.G.S.

---

* At the meeting held at Dury at 11 p.m. on Sunday, 24th March, between Pétain, Haig, and Lawrence certain statements were made by Pétain which showed clearly that his intention was, in the event of the German attacks on Amiens making progress, to order the French troops, which were assembling at Montdidier with the object of securing the connection with the British, to take a south-westerly direction of retreat to cover Paris. The accuracy of Haig's interpretation of Pétain's statement was subsequently questioned by Pétain in 1920. In correspondence Haig, in agreement with Lawrence, gave his interpretation of Pétain's statement as follows:

'As regards what passed between us at Dury on the evening of Sunday, 24th March 1918, the meeting took the form of a verbal discussion regarding the situation. From this discussion I reached the conclusion that while you were prepared loyally to help to the greatest possible extent, you retained the view that the main German attack was yet to be delivered, that it would be delivered against the French front, probably in Champagne, that in such an eventuality you might be obliged to make dispositions to cover Paris as that would be your primary care; and that should the Germans continue to advance successfully on Amiens, the French forces which were at that time collecting about Montdidier would be given a south-westerly direction for their retreat.'

This interpretation was sent to Pétain by post on 25th December 1920 and evidently agreed by him, for he never questioned its accuracy. It formed the basis of Haig's immediate action.

arrived and discussed the whole question with Sir Douglas Haig and the Chief of the General Staff. The result of these discussions was that it was agreed that the only way to get the French to act quickly and to prevent the Allied armies from being separated was to bring Foch in as Commander-in-Chief. Sir Douglas Haig pressed for this conclusion. It was arranged to hold a conference with the French authorities at Doullens at 12 noon on the following day, the 26th. The conference took place as arranged.

It was obvious that the British armies could expect little help from the French, and, in view of General Pétain's attitude on the 24th, very strenuous steps had to be taken to denude our armies in the north and accept very considerable risks to reinforce our right at the point of junction with the French. A further attempt must be made to get the French to co-operate more decisively. The first conference at Doullens was composed of army commanders, Sir Douglas Haig and the Chief of the General Staff. The Commander-in-Chief explained the situation and heard the views of the army commanders upon the actual or possible enemy action on their own fronts. Orders were issued to the 1st and 2nd Armies to extend the front of divisions in the line to permit of troops being withdrawn for use elsewhere. General Plumer was confident of being able to effect great economy in this way and to send at least three divisions south within the next ten days.

This meeting was concluded when these arrangements had been made, and meeting No. 2 was held which was composed of the same people with the Chief of the Imperial General Staff and Lord Milner in addition. The situation on the army front was explained to the Secretary of State, and he was fully informed of the steps taken to meet it.

Later a third meeting was held at which the following were present:

M. Poincaré	Sir Douglas Haig
M. Clemenceau	Chief of the General Staff
General Foch	Chief of the Imperial General Staff
General Pétain	Lord Milner
General Weygand	General Montgomery.

It was agreed that Amiens must be covered at all costs and the best way to do this was discussed at length. M. Clemenceau at first drafted a resolution appointing General Foch to co-ordinate the operations of the Allied detachments about Amiens, but eventually, on Sir Douglas Haig's advice, General Foch was given command of all the French and British troops in France and Flanders, and ordered to take over his duties on the spot. After the events at Dury on the 24th, * it had become certain that the only way to get the French to act would be to appoint a Frenchman as Commander-in-Chief of the Allied Forces. General Foch repeatedly announced himself confident of not only covering the Channel ports but also Paris and maintaining the connection between the Allied armies. It was further agreed by all present that the urgent matter was to accelerate the movement of the French troops to the battlefield.

The situation began to be easier and to stabilize at the end of March. The German attack on Arras on the 28th March, which was heavily repulsed by the 1st Army, did much to restore the situation. Other subsequent attacks were also repulsed. The weak and tender spot was astride the Somme opposite Amiens where heavy and continuous fighting took place.

French troops arrived slowly, and the point of junction between the Allies established itself south of the River Somme.

The actual point of junction was fixed as the River Luce,

---

* Note on the movements of General the Hon. Sir Herbert Lawrence, Chief of the General Staff at G.H.Q., between Saturday, 23rd March, and Tuesday, 26th March 1918, both dates inclusive:

Saturday, 23rd March   Lawrence accompanied Haig to meet Pétain at Dury at 4 p.m.

Sunday, 24th March   Lawrence at 5th Army Headquarters all the afternoon (in telephone communication with Davidson, who was with Haig at G.H.Q.). Lawrence also visited the 19th and 8th Corps and spent some time with General Fayolles, commanding French troops. Lawrence met Haig at 3rd Army Headquarters at 8 p.m. and thence accompanied Haig to meet Pétain at Dury at 11 p.m.

Monday, 25th March   Lawrence with Haig to Dury to meet Clemenceau and Pétain, but the latter did not turn up.

Tuesday, 26th March   Lawrence with Haig to Doullens at noon to meet military and civil authorities in conferences resulting in the appointment of Foch to take control of operations on the Western Front.

although the French had originally agreed to take over to the River Somme. The British 5th Army reverted to the command of Sir Douglas Haig and was gradually to be brought into reserve to be refitted in the Somme valley.

The Allied front from the 1st April was considerably longer than before, owing to the deep salient formed about Montdidier which had been caused by the rapid advance of the enemy and the lack of resisting power of the French. The former in reality marched until they were out of reach of their supplies.

Further conferences were held at Abbeville on the 29th and 30th March, and at Dury on 1st April, at which Sir Douglas Haig, the Chief of the General Staff, General Foch and M. Clemenceau were present, to settle details of the French co-operation and to hasten the arrival of the French troops, which was proceeding very slowly.

The position assigned to General Foch at the Doullens conference was not at once wholeheartedly recognized at French G.Q.G., and it became necessary to define more clearly his position as Generalissimo on the Western Front.

Accordingly a conference was held at Beauvais on 3rd April at which Sir Douglas Haig, General Foch, General Bliss, General Pershing, General Sir H. Wilson, M. Clemenceau, Mr. Lloyd George, Mr. Graham Thompson, and Brigadier-General Spears were present. The Governments of England and France and the United States agreed, on the suggestion of Sir Douglas Haig, to entrust to General Foch 'the strategical direction of military operations. The Commanders-in-Chief of the British, French and American Armies will have full control of the tactical action of their respective armies. Each Commander-in-Chief will have the right of appeal to his Government if, in his opinion, the army is endangered by reason of any order received from General Foch.'

At this date the French front was free from all pressure or attack of any kind, and it was obvious and agreed by the French Headquarters that none was likely to take place. But great difficulty was experienced in getting the French either to counter-attack, relieve any portion of our front, or even send any troops to support our centre about Arras–Bethune, which

H

had been considerably weakened by the force of the enemy's attacks.

Generals Foch and Pétain assured Sir Douglas Haig on the 3rd that a French counter-attack would be launched 'in the next few days' south of Montdidier, but this never materialized.

After a meeting at Aumale on 7th April, at which Generals Foch and Weygand, Field-Marshal Sir D. Haig, the Chief of the General Staff, and General Clive were present, General Foch at last agreed that the French 1st Army on our right should try and retake the line Demuin–Aubercourt which they had lost, and that four French infantry divisions and three cavalry divisions should be concentrated south-west of Amiens. Little or no result was obtained from this minor counter-attack with a few companies, and the French continued to lose small sectors of ground which caused much anxiety to the British troops on their left.

It was evident that the French Government, in spite of their protestations of agreement upon the strategical necessity of maintaining the connection between the French and British Armies, were chiefly concerned about covering Paris, and were bringing considerable pressure to bear upon Foch. It is probable that he was also experiencing much opposition to his plans from General Pétain and the Headquarter Staff of the French Army, who disliked his appointment.

There were two methods of affording relief to the exhausted British Army, viz., either by relief or by counter-attack. General Foch would undertake neither, but apparently preferred to wait on events and manipulate a handful of French divisions in reserve.

On this date the battle broke out again in full force with the delivery of a heavy German attack in the Lys valley. The Portuguese troops gave way and the flank of our troops to the north became exposed, thereby causing a breach in the front and the retirement of the whole line in the valley.

At a meeting at Beaurepaire on the 9th April,* at which

---

* Brigadier-General Sir James Edmonds, late Official Historian, states on page 306 of his *History of World War I:—*
Haig begged Foch to put four divisions in Reserve behind the Second Army

Sir Douglas Haig, Generals Foch and Weygand, General Sir H. Wilson, the Chief of the General Staff and General Davidson† were present, General Foch refused again to take over any part of the British line, but agreed to place the four French divisions referred to before with their heads on the Somme between Amiens and Picquigny ready to move north if required. This arrangement was quite inadequate, and when the German attack between Armentières–Bethune developed on the 10th April, Sir Douglas Haig wrote to General Foch again insisting upon the necessity of the French taking a more active part in the battle which had now continued since the 21st March. On the night of the 10th, General Foch came to Beaurépaire and said that he had at last made up his mind that the main German attack was being delivered against the British Army, and that he would move a large French force to take part in what he called the 'battaile d'Arras.' Nothing however was done, although Sir Douglas Haig wrote again to General Foch on the 11th and 14th April pointing out that the British troops were getting fast worn out, that the French were practically not engaged, and that it was urgently necessary either to take over some of our line in the south or to reinforce us in the north.

By the 15th April, French troops began to arrive by rail and road in the area of the 2nd Army and were placed under the

between St Omer and Dunkirk, but the General in Chief offered only one Cavalry Corps and that did not arrive until the 19th. He was resolute against taking over any of Haig's frontage; the British Army must hold on where it stood, for, he said, the French Army, after the events of 1917, was not yet fit to take over in a defensive battle of the present nature. To encourage his troops Haig was driven to the extremity of words and on 11th April he issued an order of the day. It ended with the call: 'There is no other course open to us but to fight it out. Every position must be held to the last man. There must be no retirement. With our backs to the wall, and believing in the justice of our cause, each one of us must fight on to the end. The safety of our homes and the freedom of mankind alike depend upon the conduct of each one of us at this critical moment.'

† During April I was constantly being sent to Foch to press him to send French troops to take some part in the battle, but he systematically refused, saying always to me, 'C'est la bataille du Nord,' with a shrug of his shoulders. After a few interviews he reluctantly admitted that the battle of the north was a British battle and not a French battle, and that it must be so, seeing that he was unwilling to put the French to the test of a defensive battle. This corroborates what the Official Historian reported above. I reported my interviews and these reports proved Foch to have been right in his judgement—for on the 25th April the French lost Mount Kemmel, a strong feature of much importance, and a day or two later the 'Scherpenberg.'—J. H. D.

command of General Plumer to hold the Kemmel sector. On the 25th April, Kemmel was captured by the Germans, and the French counter-attack on the 26th to retake the ground was a failure.

On the 27th April, at a conference at Abbeville at which M. Clemenceau, Lord Milner and the C.I.G.S. were present, General Foch said he thought the German attacks were weakening and that he felt confident of being able to cover both Paris and the Channel ports.

From the foregoing it will be seen that between the 21st March and the 15th April the French did practically nothing and took no part in the fighting. For a period of twenty-one days the British armies sustained the whole weight of the German attack by 106 divisions.

When finally General Foch agreed to relieve with French troops our worn-out divisions in the Kemmel sector, and the German attack was renewed on this front, those French troops lost one of the strongest positions on our front and made no effort to retake it.

The British armies in France had withstood the first and heaviest onslaughts of the German armies during the period 21st March to the end of April, and were consequently seriously reduced in strength, some eight divisions having been disbanded and the remainder for the most part below establishment. Undoubtedly the Germans also had suffered in their great efforts.

About the end of April, five British divisions (9th Corps), just reconstituted and badly in need of training and rest, were handed over to the French to be placed in a quiet sector, the French having dispatched a number of divisions both in rear of the British right and in the north to strengthen the Flanders front.

General Foch, throughout this period (April and May), repeatedly expressed the view that the enemy would resume an attack on a large scale on the front Arras–Amiens–Montdidier, and he did not consider that the operations in Flanders were of importance or that any attack would materialize south of Montdidier. All dispositions were made accordingly.

Both the view expressed and the dispositions made proved to be erroneous, with the following results:

(a) The enemy never delivered an attack on the Arras–Amiens–Montdidier front, and the Allied reserves in this area were gradually withdrawn to meet the situation elsewhere.

(b) The quiet part of the front selected by French G.Q.G. for the five British divisions referred to above to rest, train and refit, was the Aisne front west of Rheims, notwithstanding that Sir Douglas Haig had previously called General Foch's attention to the risk of placing tired divisions to hold a front against which the enemy had already completed his preparations for concentrating a force for assault. Major-General Davidson* (the M.G.G.S., Operations, G.H.Q.) also attended a meeting at General Foch's Headquarters at Sarcus early in May and expressed this view and the anxiety felt regarding the location of these British divisions. He was, however, assured by General Weygand and General de Barescut that the front selected was suitable and quiet. At this very moment a heavy attack on the Aisne front was impending and was actually delivered on the 27th May, with the result that the five divisions (8th, 19th, 25th, 21st, 50th), raw and weak as they were, were crushed. These divisions were eventually pulled out and sent to the mouth of the River Somme to refit or be broken up.

(c) During May and June the Crown Prince Ruprecht's reserves were, generally speaking, kept intact opposite the British front. In the Appreciation of the Situation issued by the British General Staff for the week ending 11th May it was stated that 'the enemy is preparing to renew his attacks on

---

* I had some days earlier protested to the French authorities against the selection of the Chemin des Dames front line as a suitable locality for our five exhausted divisions to rest and refit. Both the French and we knew that this front had been prepared by the Germans for an attack which seemed to be imminent. No attention, however, was paid to these protests. On the 27th May the Germans struck, thrusting back the French 45th Division on our left with the result that the British had to swing back to form a flank on the east of the bulge.

The Germans claimed 45,000 prisoners. Henceforward Foch generally gave way to Haig's views and proposals 'and adopted them.'—J. H. D.

the Scherpenberg–Mont des Cats Ridges.' This proved to be correct as, on advancing later over this ground, it was found that the Germans had dumped large quantities of ammunition, especially trench mortar ammunition, in their front line, with the obvious object of delivering a great attack to capture the hills Mont Noir, Mont Rouge, and Mont des Cats, and thence move on to the northern Channel ports.

The view held by the British General Staff was that the enemy, having struck in the centre with a considerable measure of success but without separating the Allies, intended to attack the flanks in Flanders and on the Aisne with the object of drawing off the Allied reserves and then repeat the decisive blow in the centre. The fighting which resulted in great losses in both of these flank attacks obliged the enemy to use up a large part of his reserves which otherwise would have been available for delivering a vigorous blow in the centre in the hope of gaining a decision.

By the end of June the Crown Prince's reserves were to a large extent used up, whereas Prince Ruprecht's reserves were more or less intact. During June and at the beginning of July, General Foch was becoming anxious about the Compiègne–Chateau-Thierry–Rheims front, and began to draw away his detachment in Flanders under De Mitry to the south to reinforce the French front, thus weakening the British front in Flanders by some eight divisions.

This situation was somewhat disturbing in the circumstances described above, for evidence of a heavy hostile attack in Flanders continued to accumulate.

An interesting point had arisen during the latter part of April in regard to the general distribution of the Allied troops in France and Flanders. The British armies had been heavily engaged and were exhausted. French reserves had been moved north behind the British right and had relieved certain British divisions in Flanders. British divisions exhausted had been brought out of line to rest and refit. It was obvious that if this state of affairs were to continue there would be too many troops behind the British front, although the bulk of them would be exhausted and unfit to fight, while the French front would be unduly denuded of reserves. The only remedy was a *roulement* of British divisions on the French front. This, Marshal Foch was anxious to carry out, and, if necessary, to cause an intermixture of French and British troops along the front.

A telegram from the War Office on the 19th April (No. 56739) showed the anxiety of the War Cabinet lest the British armies should lose their identity, pointing out that such a procedure was contrary to Lord Kitchener's 'Charter' No. 121/7711 of 26th December 1915, and presuming that the Field-Marshal Commanding-in-Chief would refuse to accept Marshal Foch's suggestion.

There was, however, no alternative; a *roulement* was essential, but it was unfortunate that the French authorities should have selected a battlefront (Aisne) in which to carry out the first *roulement* of British divisions. Fortunately, no further *roulement* was necessary as events turned out, but had it been necessary it was decided to carry out the *roulement* in blocks of divisions under British commanders as a temporary expedient, so as to avoid as far as possible the disintegration of the British forces.

The question of Lord Kitchener's 'Charter of instructions' had, however, been raised, and its application in present circumstances. This matter was referred to the War Office, and a further letter of instructions was received on the 22nd June by the Field-Marshal Commanding-in-Chief, the main points being:—

(*a*) If the Allied Commander-in-Chief issued instructions which in the Field-Marshal Commanding-in-Chief's opinion would, if carried out, imperil the British Army, the latter should appeal to the British Government.

(*b*) Any *roulement* of British troops to the French front must be temporary, and they should rejoin the main body of the British forces as early as possible.

Thus, as pointed out earlier, although an Allied Commander-in-Chief issues orders to the British Commander, the latter is in fact, responsible for the safety of the British forces. His safeguard is appeal or protest against the orders issued by Higher Command, a considerable source of possible friction and an added anxiety to the British Commander-in-Chief. This must be particularly so since the instrument for the defeat of Germany was the British Army; and, in the anxiety and endeavour to defeat the enemy, too frequent, unfair and impossible demands and instructions were issued to the British Commander-in-Chief with which he was not always able to comply, as will be seen later.

During the period of the enemy's attacks, certain American units were attached for instruction to the British forces, but, apart from the moral support they afforded, they were never employed in the defensive battle. All except two divisions were eventually removed to the French front. It had been hoped to incorporate some ten American divisions in the British armies for training for a considerable period and these would have been of great value for defence seeing that the Crown Prince Ruprecht's reserves were apparently not considerably reduced during the months of May, June and early July and constituted a potent threat on the British front. During this period, however, not only were all the American divisions except two removed to the French front, and all French troops withdrawn, but a demand was made by Marshal Foch to locate a British corps astride the Somme River. Sir Douglas Haig appealed to the British Government. A meeting on this subject was held in Paris on the 7th June at which Lord Milner and M. Clemenceau were present in addition to the Field-Marshal Commanding-in-Chief, the C.I.G.S. and Marshal Foch. Sir Douglas Haig's protest against the dangerous reduction of troops on the British front was discussed, but without result.

A German attack was evidently being prepared against the Ypres–Hazebrouck front, subsequent evidence proving this to be so, but owing probably to the demoralizing fire of our artillery, combined with the trend of events elsewhere, this attack never materialized. Considerable anxiety was, however, felt on the subject and up to the middle of July Marshal Foch's attention was frequently directed to the danger involved by his action. He was, however, more anxious about the French front and for reasons which will soon become apparent.

CHAPTER VIII

The British Offensive of 8th August 1918 to the Armistice

Being an extract from a document entitled *Operations on the Western Front 1916–18* (pages 67 to 73) and deals with the great counter-offensive launched against the German Army by the British on 8th August 1918 and which led up through a series of victories, including the assault on the Hindenburg Line, to the Armistice on the 11th November 1918.

The document was drawn up by the General Staff at G.H.Q., revised by the Chief of the General Staff, and subsequently approved by the Field-Marshal Commanding-in-Chief.

ON the 11th July, the Field-Marshal being in England, * the Chief of the General Staff (Sir H. Lawrence) received a message that General Foch would be glad to see him as soon as possible at his Headquarters at Bonbon. Leaving Montreuil on

---

*Note by Sir Douglas Haig regarding his movements in England at this time:

Friday, 12th July   10.30 a.m. I visited Lord Milner (Secretary of State for War) at his house, 17 Great College Street, by appointment and discussed the situation.

4 p.m. I visited 10 Downing Street:
   Present: Prime Minister (Mr. L. George).
                Lord Milner.
                C.I.G.S. (General Sir H. Wilson).
                Colonel Sir M. Hankey.

9.45 p.m. General Davidson arrived at Eastcott with letter from General Lawrence (he received it from the K.M. at the station). General Lawrence reports all quiet on our front, but 'Foch believes big attack to be impending on Chateau-Thierry–Chalons front.'

Saturday, 13th July   Foch has made up his mind that main attack will fall on French east of Rheims. Our General Staff fear enemy is preparing to put in a small attack against the French, while his main blow is delivered elsewhere.

the 12th, the Chief of the General Staff arrived at Bonbon at 3 p.m., when Foch gave him the following outline of the situation as he saw it.

He was convinced that the Germans were about to attack the French front in great strength east and west of Rheims, and was apprehensive that the attack might spread even farther east into the Argonne. In spite of the fact, which he acknowledged, that Prince Ruprecht's reserve group of divisions about Douai and Valenciennes was still opposite the British front, he considered that the enemy could attack with a force of sufficient strength to endanger his position. He therefore asked for four British divisions to be moved, two south of the Somme and two astride the river, to ensure the connection between the French and British Armies about Amiens and to enable him to move four French divisions farther east on to his right flank. This was agreed to and the orders were issued by telephone on the spot. General Foch further informed the Chief of the General Staff that if the Germans did not attack before the 18th he proposed to launch the attack which by his orders General Pétain had prepared on the west flank of the Chateau-Thierry salient.

On the morning of the 13th the Chief of the General Staff called at 4th Army Headquarters and ordered General Rawlinson to prepare plans at once for an attack east of Amiens; his army would be reinforced for this purpose. Further details and orders would be sent after the Chief of the General Staff had seen the Commander-in-Chief.

On reaching G.H.Q., a message from General Foch had arrived saying that the situation demanded that the four British divisions asked for the day before should be placed unreservedly at his disposal for employment with the French Army and that four more divisions should be dispatched to take their place.

The dispatch of the first four divisions and a corps headquarters under Lieut.-General Sir A. Godley was agreed to and the first two divisions of the second series were ordered to move. On Sir Douglas Haig's return on the 14th this action was approved, and a meeting arranged with General Foch for the 18th. On the 15th the German attack east and west of Rheims was delivered. The Commander-in-Chief and the Chief of the

General Staff met General Foch this day at Mouchy, and Sir Douglas Haig decided that the circumstances warranted the dispatch of the four divisions formed into the 22nd Corps and of four more divisions to replace them astride the Somme.

On hearing of this decision, and in view of the fact that the Crown Prince Ruprecht's reserves were more or less untouched and that a hostile attack was known to be prepared in Flanders, the War Cabinet were greatly perturbed and dispatched General Smuts at once to see Sir Douglas Haig on the subject and ascertain his views as to whether it would be advisable for the British Government to interfere. Sir Douglas Haig comforted General Smuts and said that he was prepared to take the risk involved and realized fully that if the dispositions proved to be wrong the blame would rest with him, Sir Douglas Haig, and, on the other hand, if the dispositions proved right, the credit would lie with General Foch. With this the Government could be well satisfied.*

On the 18th July the French and Americans counter-attacked between Soissons and Chateau-Thierry, and on the 20th the British 22nd Corps became involved in the fighting in this area which lasted until the end of the month.

On the 23rd July, Sir Douglas Haig and the Chief of the General Staff met General Pershing in Paris, and on the 24th proceeded to Bonbon. General Foch and the Field-Marshal first discussed the situation on the British front; Generals Lawrence and Weygand were also present. It was agreed to proceed as soon as possible with certain operations east of Amiens in which the British 4th and French 1st Armies would be involved. Subsequently, General Foch presided at a conference which was attended by Sir Douglas Haig, General Pershing, General Pétain, General Buat, General Weygand, and the Chief of the General Staff. The French and American counter-attack commenced on the 18th had been a decided success and the great German attack had definitely failed. General Foch now explained his views as to the necessity for

---

* See Chapter X. Smuts only remained at G.H.Q. for an hour or so and returned at once with a letter from Haig to the Prime Minister accepting full responsibility.

regaining the initiative and passing to the offensive, and asked the British, French and American Armies to prepare plans for local offensives with definite objectives of a limited nature. It would depend upon the measure of success which might be obtained whether such success could be more fully exploited before winter set in. The time had come to pass from the defensive to the offensive and the following operations would be taken in hand as soon as possible:—

1. With the object of freeing the Paris–Avricourt railway in the Marne area.
2. With the object of freeing the Paris–Amiens railway.
3. With the object of freeing the Paris–Avricourt railway in the Commercy area by reducing the St. Mihiel salient.

Other operations in the British area, such as the capture of Kemmel, combined with an operation in the direction of La Bassée, would have the effect of reducing the salient in the Lys valley and providing for the safety of the Bruay coalmines. These had already been the subject of correspondence between General Foch and Sir Douglas Haig.

Information was also required regarding the strength of the several allied armies on the 1st January and 1st April of next year.

On the 28th July, General Foch put the French 1st Army, commanded by General Debeney, under Sir Douglas Haig's orders for Operation 2 mentioned above.

Sir Douglas Haig had come to the conclusion that the Amiens operation should take precedence over any other offensive to be undertaken by the British armies, as being the most important and the most likely to give good results if successful.

It was settled to reinforce the 4th Army with the Canadian Corps, and also with two of the British divisions which were in readiness astride the Somme to move to the assistance of the French. In order to deceive the enemy, Canadian battalions were put into the front line on the Kemmel front, corps headquarters were prepared, and casualty clearing stations were conspicuously erected in this area, and great activity especially of wireless and tanks was maintained on the 1st Army front. General Horne was also directed to make detailed plans in an ostentatious manner by the Canadian Corps for capturing Orange Hill and Monchy-le-Preux east of Arras.

On the 5th August Sir Douglas Haig had a final conference at 4th Army Headquarters, at which General Rawlinson, General Debeney, General Kavanagh, and the Chief of the General Staff were present.

The Canadian Corps had been moved into position by night and had been kept carefully concealed, as also had the assembly of the Cavalry Corps which had been allocated to the 4th Army. If, as we hoped, the infantry and tanks succeeded in breaking the enemy line east and south-east of Villers Bretonneux, an opportunity for the use of the Cavalry Corps would occur, and detailed arrangements for their passage through the infantry were carefully worked out.

The attack was launched on the 8th August and was a success from the start, the enemy being completely surprised. The enemy line was broken, the cavalry passed through, and by the 11th August our line was in front of Chaulnes–Roye with the railway junction at Chaulnes under our gunfire. 21,850 prisoners and 400 guns were captured, the Amiens–Paris railway disengaged, and the connection between the French and British Armies definitely assured.

The position occupied by the enemy on the line Chaulnes–Roye was a very strong one and very thoroughly prepared. On the afternoon of the 10th August, the Field-Marshal, in the course of a visit to the Headquarters, 32nd Division, east of Le Quesnel, personally satisfied himself that the enemy's opposition had really stiffened.

On the night of the 12th August, Marshal Foch came to British Advanced Headquarters and requested Sir Douglas Haig to attack this position at once and to endeavour to secure Peronne and the crossings of the Somme south of that place, as well as the high ground to the east of it.

Further reconnaissances on the 13th showed the strength of the Chaulnes–Roye position, and on the 15th Sir Douglas Haig addressed a letter to Marshal Foch in which he stated that he was not prepared to make the attack suggested. He proposed to transfer the front of attack to the north of the Somme; that the

3rd Army would operate in the direction of Bapaume, in co-operation with the 4th Army towards Peronne on the south of the Somme; that eventually the 1st Army would prolong the north flank of the attack as far as the Scarpe. Marshal Foch objected very strongly to this proposal, and a meeting was arranged at Sarcus between Sir Douglas Haig, Marshal Foch, the Chief of the General Staff and General Weygand. The discussion was heated, and finally Sir Douglas Haig peremptorily refused to attack the Chaulnes–Roye position. After such conversation, Marshal Foch accepted the British proposal and promised to attack with the French Army over a wide front in order to facilitate the attack of the 3rd Army, which was to take place about the 20th. The French 1st Army returned to General Pétain's command.*

The attack of the 3rd Army began on the morning of the 21st August, on the front Puisieux–Moyenneville, and was carried out by the 4th and 6th Corps. It was recognized that the enemy position immediately in front of these corps was probably only an outpost position and that the main line of resistance would be found to be along the Amiens–Albert railway and the high ground east of it. This proved to be the case, and the 22nd August was employed to get the troops and guns into position for the main attack while the 3rd or left Corps of the 4th Army improved its position between the Ancre and the Somme.

The battle was continued on the 23rd by the 6th, 4th and 5th Corps of the 3rd Army in the order named from the north, and by the 3rd Corps of the 4th Army. On subsequent days till the 31st the whole of the 3rd and 4th Armies presssed forward with greatest vigour, driving the enemy before them, capturing Bapaume, Peronne, and many other places, together with 34,250 prisoners and 240 guns.

By the 24th it had become clear that the moment had arrived for extending the front of attack northwards to the River Scarpe and that the 1st Army should co-operate with the 3rd and 4th Armies in the general advance. The Canadian Corps had been transferred to the 1st Army and placed in the line

*See Chapter X.

south of the River Scarpe, and in conjunction with the 17th Corps, 3rd Army, on its right on the 26th August attacked and carried Monchy-le-Preux. Continuing their successful advance, the 1st Army came into line with the 3rd Army, and by the 3rd September had captured 18,850 prisoners and 200 guns. This last advance included the brilliant operation of breaking the hinge of the Drocourt–Queant line about Queant, in which action the Canadian and 17th Corps particularly distinguished themselves (2nd September).

Meanwhile, on the 31st August, a cipher telegram was received by Sir Douglas Haig from the C.I.G.S. War Office, cautioning the former against incurring heavy losses in attacks on the Hindenburg Line and that such losses would be a source of anxiety to the War Cabinet.* Instructions had also been received by Sir Douglas Haig from Marshal Foch for the British armies to continue their operations with determination and without delay on the front St. Quentin–Cambrai, that is, to break through the Hindenburg Line. This confliction of direct orders and indirect suggestions was difficult to harmonize, and left Sir Douglas Haig in the same predicament as in the case of General Smuts' visit, referred to above. Sir Douglas Haig, however, as in the case of General Smuts' visit, was prepared to take the risk, accept the responsibility, and act according to his judgement.

During this period, i.e. the end of August and beginning of September, a discussion arose between Marshal Foch and Sir Douglas Haig regarding the strategical plan upon which the future operations should be based. As stated above, Marshal Foch's original conception was of a limited nature, i.e. operations to be conducted so as to free certain strategical railways.

Copy of cipher telegram:
Sir D. Haig (from General Sir H. Wilson).
85HW 31.8.18.

Personal just a line of caution in regard to incurring heavy losses in attacks on Hindenburg Line as opposed to losses when driving the enemy back to that line.

I do not mean to say that you have incurred such losses but I know the War Cabinet would become anxious if we received heavy punishment in attacking the Hindenburg line without success.

103

Events had, thanks to the successful operations of the British forces, moved so rapidly that it seemed necessary to enlarge the scope of offensive and combine the various attacks so as to inflict a decisive defeat on the enemy. Marshal Foch's plan then was for the American Army to pass from the attack on the St. Mihiel salient, which took place on the 12th September, to an offensive against the Briey ironfields, the French to attack in Champagne, the British to attack on the St. Quentin–Cambrai front, while an Allied attack was to be carried out in Flanders to free the Belgian coast. These attacks appeared to Sir Douglas Haig to be eccentric and lack co-ordination and cohesion, and in corresponding with Marshal Foch he pointed out the desirability of altering the direction of the American attack to the direction of Mézières with its right on the Meuse.

On the 9th September, after meeting General Foch at Cassel to settle the details for an Allied advance on Ghent, Sir Douglas Haig proceeded to London and next day saw the Secretary of State for War at the War Office. He informed Lord Milner in the presence of his C.G.S. (General Lawrence) that he (the Commander-in-Chief) considered that the character of the war had changed owing to the extraordinary series of victories gained by the British Army in France, and that in his opinion 'a decision might be obtained in the very near future.' Instead of heavy guns, light troops, mounted men, lorries and everything which would increase mobility should be sent at once.

Some days were now required to reorganize and improve the rear communications, and it was not till the 18th September that the 3rd and 4th Armies resumed their advance in order to bring the latter army and the right of the 3rd Army within striking distance of the Hindenburg Line along the St. Quentin Canal. The action on the 18th and 19th September was completely successful and resulted in the capture of the objective aimed at, together with 11,750 prisoners and 150 guns. The enemy still, however, held in force a strong position west of their main line of resistance, the Hindenburg Line.

Between the 19th and 27th September there was much local hard fighting along the army fronts, and our general position was steadily improved in preparation for the next attack on a large scale.

Havrincourt, captured by the 6th Corps on the 12th September, was held against repeated counter-attacks in great force. This village was essential to the successful prosecution of the attack upon Bourlon Wood and Marcoing.

Although the 4th Army was very nearly in a position to launch its attack upon the Hindenburg Line, the 1st and 3rd Armies were still some way from their objective. The task of the 4th Army included the capture of the tunnel through which the St. Quentin Canal passes. This tunnel had been fortified and prepared for two years for an occasion like the present, and a prolonged bombardment was necessary to make certain of carrying the position by assault.

The attack was therefore fixed for the 27th September, on which day a bombardment was commenced upon the whole front of the 1st, 3rd and 4th Armies, but only the 1st and 3rd Armies attacked. On the north the 1st Army forced a passage over the Canal du Nord and captured Bourlon Wood. Their advance brought them into the outskirts of Cambrai and on to the ground north of the town. The 3rd Army captured the ridges south of Havrincourt and effected a crossing over the canal at Marcoing, while everywhere they seized the high ground on the east of this obstacle. Fighting continued throughout the next day, the position north of Cambrai was improved and the bridgehead at Marcoing widened. At dawn on the 29th the 4th Army attacked and brilliantly carried the whole of the Hindenburg Line of the canal south of Bellenglise as well as the tunnel referred to before. Some days were to elapse before the tunnel and its defences were thoroughly cleared, when the capture of the high ground about La Terriere enabled the 5th and 4th Corps of the 3rd Army to cross and finally occupy the whole of the Hindenburg Line, including the Beaurevoir reserve line. The 46th Division, which attacked the canal south of Bellenglise by swimming, on rafts and with life-belts, and stormed the position on the eastern side, captured over 4,000 prisoners and forty guns. The strength of the position was incredible and the performance a most notable one. In the

I

centre of the 4th Army, two United States divisions (the 27th and 30th) attacked over the tunnel and advanced with great gallantry. Moving forward too fast, they apparently neglected to clear the tunnel and suffered heavy casualties. The Australian Corps which followed them took some days to clear effectually the tunnel and fully occupy the ground beyond.

In these operations from the 27th September to the 30th, 30,500 prisoners were captured besides 380 guns, and the whole of the Hindenburg Line completely broken north of St. Quentin.

Full advantage was immediately taken of these important successes and the situation exploited, so that by the 9th October the whole of the main railway line St. Quentin–Busigny–Cambrai was in our possession and our front advanced as far east as Le Cateau. We were thus in possession of an important lateral double line of railway. This, however, had been so completely destroyed by the enemy that it was evident that some time must elapse before the communications were restored, arrangements for which had been put in hand at once.

Until these communications were restored, it would not be possible to operate much farther afield on the Oise–Scheldt front, as railheads were becoming too distant. A series of operations were, however, undertaken to reach the line of the Sambre and Oise Canal–western edge of the Mormal Forest–Valenciennes, and these were practically completed by the 24th October.

During the month of October the American and French forces were to operate northwards with their right on the Meuse in the direction of Mézières, i.e. in a concentric direction and in combination with the British attack on the Cambrai–St. Quentin front, while the British 2nd Army with the Belgians and a few French troops continued to exploit the success already gained on September 28th by driving forward in the direction of Ghent.

The Franco-American attack started well but was soon held up, in the case of the Americans by lack of experience and disorganization of their rearward services, in the case of the French by other causes.

The British successes in the centre were, however, of such a magnitude that they caused the enemy's resisting power to weaken on other parts of the front, with the result that the Americans at the end of October began to make further progress, reaching Mézières before the Armistice was signed, while the French followed up the retreating enemy in the neighbourhood of Laon.

Meanwhile the British communications were restored sufficiently to enable a general attack to be carried out on the 4th November towards the general objective line Avesnes–Maubeuge–Mons. This attack was completely successful, the enemy routed and pursued, and the general objective line was reached on the 10th November. The Armistice being signed on the 11th November put an end to operations.

During all this period, from the 8th August onwards, much difficulty had been experienced by the 4th Army on its right by the tendency of the French to hang back, thus exposing a long defensive right flank. Many verbal expostulations were made both to General Debeney and to Marshal Foch on the subject, but it was quite evident that the French did not intend to move forward until our advance had threatened the flank of the Germans opposing them. This unsatisfactory state of affairs was also apparent on the left flank of the British armies.

The British 2nd Army, as may be seen from the Field-Marshal Commanding-in-Chief's dispatch dated 21st December 1918, had been *temporarily* placed under the command of the King of the Belgians (with General Degoutte as Chief of Staff) with the object of clearing the Flanders coast and reaching the line of the River Lys. The whole of these operations are described in the above-mentioned dispatch, but two points are worthy of notice, no mention being made of them in the dispatch:—

First:

The French troops sent to Flanders to co-operate with the Belgians and British did not co-operate effectively with their allies. These French troops showed little or no anxiety to attack, and, by persistently hanging back, were constantly exposing the northern flank of the British 2nd Army. Orders constantly received from Marshal Foch for the Flanders group to attack meant, in effect, that the British and

Belgians would attack and that the French would do little except to follow up where there was practically no opposition. The brunt of the fighting, therefore, fell on the British 2nd Army. Seeing that the remainder of the British forces were also attacking on a separate battle ground, the onus of the offensive operations was being placed unfairly on British shoulders, and the incidence of casualties fell out of all fair proportion on the British troops. In view of the attitude of the British Government, this rendered the Field-Marshal's position exceedingly difficult. Throughout the period from the 8th August, the perpetual cry of the Government was that no casualties were to be incurred and no operations undertaken which were dangerous.

Second:

The 2nd Army had been attached temporarily to the Flanders group for the specific object mentioned above. That object having been attained, Marshal Foch did not return the 2nd Army to the command of the Field-Marshal but continued to use it as the battering ram of the Flanders group.

At the end of October the Field-Marshal interviewed Marshal Foch and insisted on the return of the 2nd Army, but the latter refused. The matter was referred to the home authorities, and eventually after the C.I.G.S. had interviewed Marshal Foch, the latter agreed at a meeting with the Field-Marshal at Senlis on the 20th October to transfer the 2nd Army to British command. This was effected on the 4th November 1918.

CHAPTER IX

Comments

MORALE: FRENCH AND GERMAN

Napoleon made the well-known remark which has since become a platitude: 'The moral is to the physical as three is to one.' If it were true a century and a half ago, it is much more true today. With nations in arms and with the improved means of communication as there exist today, morale has its effect not only on the services or fighting front but almost equally on the civil or home front and each of these fronts has its reactions on the other and the effect is thereby increased. We have seen both as regards the French and Germans this was the case in 1916, 1917 and 1918; the conditions at the front expressed in correspondence depressed the civil population, and the hardships experienced at home tended to react on the troops.

There is substantial similarity in the progress of moral collapse in each of these armies, in France and in Germany. Both began to show deterioration of morale after the long-drawn-out, severe and costly fighting at Verdun and the Somme. It was only to be expected that France would crack first, partly because its army was the smaller and had experienced a heavier strain, but chiefly because of the psychological difference in the mental set-up of the two nations. The French are excitable, highly strung and temperamental, whereas the Germans are more stolid, more disciplined and more accustomed to order.

The tragic effect of the moral collapse in the French Army has been exposed in the preceding chapters. German morale was also running down in the winter of 1916–17, but did not take its first real downward plunge until after the triple battles of Broodseinde in September–October 1917. It recovered sharply and temporarily as in the case of the French—before the battles of the 21st March and 9th April 1918, when the *Kaiserschlacht* was unleashed as a bid for victory. But when these battles were lost, their morale reacted sharply, it slumped and three months later it had deteriorated so rapidly as to cause defeat.

We know the history of the French collapse, but here are two quotations by German authorities on the German collapse which corroborate each other. In *Frankreichs schwerste Stunde* it is stated when Hindenburg and Ludendorf

> took over command they found the Western Front in a dangerous condition of exhaustion. Not a single one of the Infantry Regiments which had been put in again and again at Verdun and on the Somme now possessed a strong cadre of old soldiers. In every battle report, and from the mouth of every Field Officer, Hindenburg and Ludendorf heard the despairing cries of the fast disappearing Infantry for material equal to that of their opponents.
>
> There is no doubt that at the end of 1916, the German soldier quitted the battlefields of Verdun and the Somme—where he had left the best of his powers—with the tragic feeling of inferiority to the Artillery and Air Force of his opponents. The German leaders were also fully aware that morale had suffered seriously under the depressing influences of the past year. On top of this came the bitterly cold winter in Germany, an icy cold wave from the Steppes of Siberia, which lasted many months. Want of coal and complete want of warm clothing sharpened the misery of winter so that it could hardly be borne.

And here again *Wissen und Wehr* (September 1924) gives an answer to why the Germans failed in March 1918.

> Involuntarily the question arises in one's mind, why did an offensive begun with such powerful forces peter out after only six or nine days?
>
> The key to the riddle must be sought in the psychological and physical conditions of the troops. The best of the old German Army lay dead on the battlefields. What had later appeared bore an ever increasing militia-like character. As time passed the picture gradually changed for the worse in proportion as the number of old peace-time officers in a unit grew smaller and as they were replaced by young fellows of the very best will, but often without sufficient knowledge. At the same time the old corps of N.C.O.s rapidly disappeared so that finally the difference between the N.C.O. and Private vanished very much to the detriment of discipline.

The tendency of the German nation was naturally to live by rote and rule; Germans are not adept at improvisation, as are the British essentially, and to a lesser extent the French. When their system broke down, they were lost without their trained and experienced leaders.

With both the French and Germans there was a steady and prolonged fall in morale, then a sharp and shortlived recovery followed by collapse, with mutiny in the case of the former and with defeat in the case of the latter.

I have little doubt that Haig visualized some such picture of moral declension as before related, but he probably had judged the progress of German declension to be more rapid than it actually was. Nevertheless he was fundamentally correct in his judgement and amply justified in his action, for his view of British morale was that it would outlast that of Germany, more particularly with the prospect of American intervention approaching.

Clearly a danger signal to the Germans was Ludendorf's 'Black Day' of the 4th October 1917 at Broodseinde and the crash feared and presaged occurred on the second 'Black Day,' the 8th August 1918, the first day of the series of battles which ended in the surrender of the German Army.

As in the past, and as in the present, so in the future, it is the man behind the gun or bomb or machine, wherever he may be, in the air, on the sea, or on the land or in the factory, that counts and determines the result. National morale requires watching and caring for throughout. Haig fully recognized its importance. All this no doubt is platitude, but it was the first time that the British Nation and Commonwealth had been faced with such a problem, on so large and national a scale, and with such far-reaching results.

SECRECY REGARDING FRENCH MORALE

In this book I have tried to probe the 'Depression Morale' of the French Army, its intensity and its cause and effect. My chief reasons were: firstly because it had such a powerful influence on Haig's plans and action from May 1917 to the end of the war, which must be taken into account in assessing his judgement; secondly there are lessons to be learned in comparing the French and German morale; thirdly the fact that the secrecy which enveloped the moral collapse of the French in April–May 1917 was so complete and effective as to create scepticism as to its reality. It is to this secrecy and consequent scepticism or suspicion in the minds of many holding relatively important and responsible positions, who would have been expected to be cognisant of the true facts, that I wish to refer for a moment.

To get an idea of the strictness of the secrecy applied by the French, one has only to take the case of General Sir Henry Wilson, who was a close friend of Foch, and had been chosen for the post of Chief of the British Mission at Nivelle's Headquarters. I have referred to the episode in Chapter II, but it would be as well to elaborate it further here. It will be recollected that the British Army had been placed for the direction of operations under Nivelle. When the French grand offensive on the Aisne failed on 16th April 1917, Nivelle shortly after was deposed and Pétain was appointed as Commander-in-Chief in his place. Wilson was therefore at French Headquarters when Pétain was commanding and Foch was Chief of the General Staff, and when the French mutinies broke out. One would have expected that Wilson would have been made acquainted with or would have made himself acquainted with the circumstance of the mutinies, but in his diary of this period, May, he gives no hint of any true conception of what was occurring in the French Army, and there is little doubt that the French Headquarters did what they could to discourage him in his efforts to find out the facts, for the British Army had by then reverted to its own British Command. At the same time Wilson had been officially informed from British sources that the British War Cabinet had only agreed to the continuation of offensive action by the British Army if the French co-operated wholeheartedly with the British in such action. The British should not fight alone. He, however, had gained the impression that the French co-operation would not amount to much, and indeed that it would certainly not be wholehearted, and, further, that there was some reason for their attitude which had not been disclosed to him. The more he probed the conditions of the French the more he suspected some trouble in their army, and the less the French High Command appreciated his enquiries.

Eventually he urged Pétain to make it clear to Haig that French co-operation would be very limited, and pressed him to do so before the British committed themselves to the launching of an offensive. Pétain found this perfectly legitimate interference by Wilson troublesome and irksome and possibly dangerous in connection with the French secret trouble, and, with the assistance of Foch, who equally found Wilson too inquisitive, got him removed from his appointment. Wilson was accordingly recalled. He had found out more than was healthy for him from the French point of view; he was anxious to prevent Haig from being drawn into the launching of an offensive without the co-operation of his ally. On the other hand, Pétain was anxious that Haig should do exactly what the British War Cabinet wanted to avoid. Wilson's attitude was perfectly proper and correct, but what he did not know was that Haig had been kept very fully informed of the French troubles, nor did he realize that, in spite of the War Cabinet restriction, Haig had come to the conclusion, under the circumstances, that the need for offensive action by the British was of more rather than of less urgency, for armies in a state of demoralization become vulnerable, and do not recover completely in a few weeks or months. Haig frequently said that his task was to keep the French in the war, but he meant to feel his way and do nothing rash.

Wilson, when he was recalled, paid a visit on his way home to his friend Rawlinson, who was in command on the Belgian coast, preparing for the projected amphibious operation which, in conjunction with the advance from the Ypres–Roulers watershed of the main armies, was intended to clear out the German submarine bases of Ostende and Zeebrugge. Rawlinson recorded that Wilson was depressed and pessimistic, but could give no reason for it.

Charteris, chief of Intelligence at G.H.Q., on 19th May recorded in his diary

> News not good today. French having very serious trouble in their own Army. Foch does not think Wilson fulfilling any useful purpose at G.Q.G. and should go. Foch wants Wilson anywhere but near himself.

Wilson's depression was due no doubt to the knowledge of the

French troubles which he had gleaned, but that knowledge was only partial, and he did not disclose anything of all this to Rawlinson. It was only after the lapse of three months that Rawlinson became acquainted with the existence of the mutinies. Charteris had received certain reports, but even he did not know the true facts until much later.

I record all this only to show that the French authorities were serious in the measures they took to prevent leakage, for that would probably have involved an enemy attack followed by defeat. Here were three senior and responsible officers, General Sir Henry Wilson, just recently attached to Pétain's Headquarters, General Sir Henry Rawlinson, commanding an army on the coast, and Brigadier-General Charteris, chief of Intelligence at Haig's Headquarters, who were unacquainted with the true facts, but should normally have been in a position to advise their chief, who in fact knew more than all of them put together.

I met very few people who referred to this demoralization; the only British officer at the French Mission who was well informed on the subject, so far as I knew, was Spears, now General Sir Edward Spears, who must have had contacts; he knew a great deal and kept his mouth shut.

I was aware of the conditions and kept informed. Although it was essential, I did not always find it easy to maintain silence. During June and July many senior officers, corps and divisional commanders passed through G.H.Q. coming from the south and moving up the Flanders front, and they nearly all asked me the same two questions—which army they were to join—2nd or 5th, and why we were going to attack in Flanders instead of in conjunction with the French? The second question was difficult to answer without some reference to the forbidden subject. They showed, however, complete and unquestioning loyalty to Haig. Indeed, I may say that I had only one objectionable experience, and that was with a contemporary, who lost his temper, and heatedly accused me of misleading Haig; I told him to go away and refused to answer his questions or argue with him. He resented my action very much as I subsequently heard. Secrecy did certainly on occasions lead to misunderstandings, hasty conclusions, gossip and criticisms which had no real foundation.

For a long time after the war there continued in certain quarters wild statements and even positive assertions, some of them by so-called experts, with the object of discrediting Haig; such, for example, that Pétain had all the time been opposed to the British offensive in Flanders in 1917, and that the French mutinies had been grosssly exaggerated and were really insignificant. I, therefore, in November 1934 sent the following letter to the Press, which reads as follows:—

I have observed from recent statements in the Press and elsewhere that Marshal Pétain, then commander-in-chief of the French armies in France, is reported to have been opposed to the British offensive in Flanders in 1917. This I know to be untrue, and I quote verbatim from a letter received by me from Lord Haig, written on 4th March 1927, on the occasion of this subject having been raised: 'I hope that the Official History will give the true story. The problem for us was how to prevent the Germans from attacking the French who were then incapable of offering an effective resistance. The mere suggestion of a pause in our attacks in the north at once brought Pétain in his train to see me and beg me to put in another effort against Passchendaele without any delay. Knowing as I did what the *rotten* state of the French Army was in 1917 (for Pétain told me more than once of his awful anxieties), I felt thankful when the winter came and the French Army was still in the field.'

Now it may seem to be a trivial matter that one word, the word '*rotten*,' was not included in the published letter; it had been deliberately omitted; and, on seeing the letter in print in the newspaper the following morning, I at once went to register my protest at the omission, as I considered it to be one more attempt to draw a veil over the condition of the French, and I knew well enough that Haig was not the man to use the word 'rotten' if he did not mean it. The French at the time in question never queried the accuracy of my letter.

I was informed that the word had been deliberately omitted lest it might give offence to the French. At the same interview an offer on my part to write a special article on the French Army, exposing its condition in 1917 and its present 1934 deep-seated weaknesses was refused for the same reason. I was troubled at this, for I was convinced that it was a mistake to suppress both knowledge and truth; such is normally an unsound policy.

Possibly I was wrong at the time in making this effort, but both Sir Herbert Lawrence and I had knowledge of the drift of French morale, mental and political, the feeling, difficult to describe, of the poilu who looked towards the east and the frontier and saw nothing but a vision of 1870–71 and 1914–17; it represented a feeling of defeatism. We felt aware of the evil effect of the defeatist Pétain with his doctrine of defence, which was gripping the army, of the Maginot Line which was drugging the army and of communism which was increasing in the Chamber of Deputies. In 1940 we were not the least surprised, though horrified, at the return of Pétain, who had threatened to run out in 1917 but was protected from it by Haig, who had tried to run out in 1918, but was prevented from it by Haig, and who was actually to run out in 1940.

I need only say that the *British Official History* deals with the French mutinies adequately, though indeed somewhat unwillingly, as though it had been dragged into this unpleasant subject as a result of the frank and convincing admission and publication of the details in the *French Official History*. Indeed, I sympathize with our historian.

I have never believed that the President of the French Republic, his Prime Minister, War Minister, Minister of the Interior, Chief of the General Staff and Commander-in-Chief were all conspiring together to mislead the British Commander-in-Chief and the British Chief of the Imperial General Staff, when they each at different times and on different occasions referred to the serious state of their own army. It is perhaps more charitable to conclude that those disbelieving critics have not read the British and French Official Histories and have taken no trouble to verify the facts.

LIAISON

I have heard Haig criticized for his optimism; this would not be objectionable if it were not associated with a further criticism that it was the outcome of ignorance of the real conditions at the front, and that he was misinformed by his staff as to those conditions. Certainly we are fortunate in being able to agree that Haig had a naturally and reasonably buoyant temperament; fortunate, I repeat, because without it he would have experienced almost insuperable difficulty in carrying on, with all his allies failing and falling out of the picture. He kept himself closely informed by continually visiting army, corps, and divisional and brigade headquarters, and by riding out to meet the troops on their way to and from the front, to visit them in their camps and billets, as well as to visit casualty clearing stations and hospitals.

He regularly received reports from his staff, and the statement is untrue that no system of liaison between G.H.Q. and the front was in force before 1918 or that it was either inadequate or out of date. It was in operation at the outbreak of the war in 1914 and it was always kept up to date. When this criticism was made in 1936, and in order to refute it, I wrote to one of the General Staff Officers who had been in the Operations Directorate at G.H.Q. in 1917, and who subsequently rose to high rank in the army and he replied to me in May 1936 to the effect that the inference to be drawn from the statement was that no liaison system was in force before 1918; that statement was incorrect for no new system was evolved in 1918, the old system of liaison had been in vogue since 1914 and it had been developed and improved as the war went on, and he added that that is what happened to every other system as the war progressed.

The five liaison officers, one for each army, were specially selected and their difficult work was carried out efficiently and appreciated by Haig.

Another criticism was that the general staff at G.H.Q. did not maintain close enough contact with 2nd Army Headquarters (Plumer) and was of little help to it during its difficult task in Flanders in 1917. To refute this seems to me to be a waste of time, but, as it was fairly widespread, I may as well put it on record as it is not without interest. On the conclusion of the Flanders offensive in 1917, Plumer and his staff with five divisions were sent hurriedly to Italy to stem the Caporetto debacle. Both he, Plumer, and his Chief of Staff, Harrington, wrote personally to me from there as follows, dated 6th January 1918: from Plumer, 'We owe you a great deal, we of the 2nd Army, for all the help you gave us, all the year, and we shall always remember very gratefully all you did for us. Good luck to you. Yours sincerely, Herbert Plumer.' From Harrington (it is unnecessary to record the first part of the letter, but it continues): 'We had a great year's work together, which I shall never forget, etc., etc.' It seems that G.H.Q. Operations and 2nd Army Headquarters had worked reasonably well together. Sir Noel Birch, Chief Artillery Adviser at G.H.Q., and I with Harrington had studied conditions on the ground, not only in regard to weather but also in relation to destruction of the terrain by artillery. I also studied them from the air on many occasions.

I also might mention here that I had incidentally happened to have spent an interesting day in mid-October 1914 marooned behind the German cavalry in the country around Passchendaele, when on a special mission with secret orders to Rawlinson to be delivered to him at Roulers on his way south from the Belgian coast with the 7th Division. Intending to motor via Poperinghe and Ypres to Roulers, I was stopped outside the former village by Belgian police, who informed me that a strong patrol of Uhlans was actually in that village and they deflected me to the north. After dodging about the country and hiding on the ridge between Ypres and Roulers most of the afternoon trying to elucidate the situation, with a certain amount of gun and rifle fire confused in most directions, I made a bolt for Roulers to the Mairie, only to find that Rawlinson had left for Ypres early that morning with his rearguard, and that German cavalry were at that moment busy billeting there; it was only by the mercy of Providence, a Rolls-Royce and an excellent Belgian chauffeur that I succeeded in getting in and out of Roulers and, making a dash for Ypres, which I reached after some vicissitudes after dusk, I delivered my message to Rawlinson. But the point of this story is that the lie of the land was deeply impressed on my mind and was valuable to me in 1917.

Information of any importance was always passed on to Haig,

who listened patiently, but I was amazed at his detailed knowledge, and his retentive memory. It is farcical to suggest that he did not know what he was doing. He knew a good deal more than most people thought.

DEFENCE OR ATTACK

I must refer to that peculiar period 1936 to 1939 when this country and France were suffering from a particularly dangerous disease, which showed its symptoms and expressed itself in articles and letters on the subject of 'Defence or Attack.' These writings attracted attention, and put briefly, the contention was that 'defence is much superior to attack.' This disease had been discovered by two experts in France, Professors Pétain and Maginot, who, working together, had mistakenly regarded it as soothing and beneficial generally; they had found that it diffused the comforting feeling that one could wage wars without moving and win battles without fighting. The deep recesses of the Maginot Line provided safety and, at the worst, the system of trenches fortified with steel and concrete pillboxes, protected by barbed wire, was preferable to fighting in the open.

Now this germ found its way across the English Channel, and immediately infected quite a number of individuals who were more expert at writing than fighting. The trouble was that it definitely acted as an opiate. The germ had been diagnosed and described by one writer in the following words:—

> The British soldier has an aptitude for defence, but not for attack, he should be trained specifically for defence; it is unnecessary to go all out in war, all we need is to convince the enemy that he cannot win, and that the purpose can be achieved by a defensive attitude.

On the outbreak of war in September 1939, this policy was apparently put into effect automatically. The combatant parties sat opposite each other, at some distance apart, imitating the ancient Chinese practice of waging war by making faces at each other, or indulging in jibes at each other through loudspeakers. There was no reason why this impressive inaction without casualties on either side, which Winston Churchill calls the twilight war, but what I prefer to call the twilight sleep, should not have continued *ad infinitum* without any result, if both sides had been like-minded. I have a recollection that 'Scrutator' had some remarks to offer on this sort of strategy. At the time the Germans were busy devouring Poland. Having digested that unfortunate country, and not believing in the popular teachings described above, they turned west and proceeded to destroy France, and very nearly inflicted a defeat on the British. But the British, being an island people, as well as alert and courageous, took to the water like ducks while the Professors Pétain and Maginot were denounced as quacks. Britain recovered in a remarkable manner, under the inspiring leadership of Winston Churchill, lived to fight another day and prove the superiority of attack.

My attention has been drawn to Churchill's *The Second World War, Vol. II*, as serialized in the *Daily Telegraph* of date 7th February 1949, under the heading for that date '*The Battle of France, Sudden Disaster*,' line 20 *et seq.*, which reads:—

> No one can understand the decisions of that period without realizing the immense authority wielded by the French military leaders, and the belief of every French officer that France had the primacy in the military art. France had conducted and carried the main weight of the terrible land fighting from 1914 to 1918.

I must refer to the two sentences in the above quotation separately. With regard to the first sentence the statement is quite true. The French had always, and frequently mistakenly, considered that they had the primacy in the military art. On this occasion what was their military art in which they had the primacy? It was the spirit of Pétain and Maginot combined, it was the superiority of defence over attack, it was the desire to fight behind or under steel and concrete, it neglected the whole value and virtue of the Maginot Line, the value of using its powerful defences to liberate the maximum number of troops as mobile reserves for offence, as a strong central reserve to meet emergency, to attack and fight offensively for the danger spot, the gap or whatever it might be. One could hardly call their action the primacy of the military art, it was the negation of military art. The reason for this is to be found in the second sentence of the above quotation, which I repeat here. 'France had conducted and carried the main weight of the terrible land fighting from 1914 to 1918.' This is a misconception. The French Army did little after their defeat on the Aisne in April 1917. The whole burden then fell on the British until the Americans began to arrive. They had lost heart at the time of the Aisne mutinies, and they had not regained it. I have little doubt that their leaders in 1939–40 suspected this or knew it.

There was defect in their leadership, it had clearly not the right spirit, nor had it the knowledge of military art. Otherwise Gamelin would have made proper offensive use of the Maginot Line, he would have organized and provided a powerful central reserve under his own hand to deal with his left flank, the gap, the obvious weak spot. He did not do so. The situation was a difficult one for the British from the outset and the whole strategy should have been thrashed out with the French. It would be no easy job, as Churchill says, but an essential one.

I will not draw further from the events of the recent war to prove the advantage and necessity of the spirit of 'attack.' Events speak for themselves. The victorious advance of our troops from Alamein and from Normandy, referred to earlier, constituted a series of major successes inspired by leaders with the offensive spirit and the inspiration of a high morale, and which, with the co-operation of the other allies, achieved final victory. All this is history, and a complete answer to the advocates of defence, which was adopted in the years preceding the war.

I must, however, revert for a moment to World War I with which I am better acquainted, which was fought under completely different conditions, and yet in spite of many difficulties and some errors proved the efficiency of attack over defence. I must refer once more to the three battles of Passchendaele of the 20th and 26th September and the 'Black Day' of 4th October 1917. Here was an enemy position prepared for defence over a period of years, heavily fortified, on open and very difficult ground, abounding in barbed wire and steel and concrete pillboxes, defending the advance to the submarine bases on the Belgian coast. Three (British and Commonwealth) attacks were separately delivered at intervals of a few days. Each was completely successful. On each occasion a succession of hostile counter-attacks was delivered over ground recently occupied by the defenders. Every counter-attack was smashed, not one succeeded in recovering a yard of ground, the damage inflicted was devastating and the defeat was as complete as it could be. Moreover, all accounts show that the enemy morale had received a very heavy blow.

The fact of the matter is that the nation that trains its army in peace on defensive lines alone is asking for trouble, asking for defeat, and deserves it. The defensive training is, in days of nations in arms, damaging not only to the army concerned, but to the national spirit. The long period of defence sustained by the German Army in 1917 at the Aisne, Arras front, Messines and Flanders had seriously damaged its morale.

Although I have dealt elsewhere with the great British attack and advance on 8th August 1918, which was the first step in a series of attacks delivered in admirably timed succession from south to north, always broadening the basis of attack until the whole British front was moving to final victory, I wish to make one comment and one quotation here.

Apart from the excellence of the plan and its development, the real reason is given by General Montgomery, Chief of Staff of the 4th Army, the day before the assault:—

> Nothing was more remarkable on the 7th August than the spirit and supreme confidence of all the troops to whatever Army they belonged. It may be said without exaggeration that so strong was this feeling, so high the morale, so fixed the determination to reach the further objective at whatever the cost, that the battle of Amiens was really won before the attack began.

He adds as a final reason that

> Nothing would shake the faith of the victorious Army in their old Commander Haig.

The army was imbued with the spirit of the attack, and possessed morale of a very high order.

During the past half-century there has been an immense increase in the power of weapons of destruction. In spite of this, or possibly because of it, there has been a growing advantage of attack over defence. This has been observable from 1870–71 to 1914–18 and again to 1939–45, and it is not due only to the psychological or moral aspect, but also to the physical and material aspect. There are and always have been certain prerequisites in attack in modern warfare. In 1870–71 there was the necessity for rigid discipline, for mobility and power of rapid manœuvre and for efficient cover provided by the fire power of gun, rifle and field gun. In 1914–18 there was cover for the attacking troops provided by the massed and concentrated fire of artillery, heavy, howitzer, field and machine-gun, poured with devastating effect on defenders, defence works and counter-attacks. In the interval 1918 to 1939 between the two wars the intrusion of air power and ground armour were becoming more evident and foreshadowing great developments of increasing importance. In 1939–45 immense advance had been made in air power. In fact it had been established at an early stage in that war that nothing of an enduring character could be achieved on the ground without command of the air to cover attacking infantry and tanks. Moreover, it was during that war that the power of the air had enabled naval battles to be fought at thousands of miles from their bases, and fleets to be maintained and supplied at such distances.

What can we expect during the next half-century, with the further development of aircraft, rockets, bombs and the power and energy which will be derived and developed from nuclear fission both in the field and in the factory. All this development seems to show that in the three media, water, land and air, the tendency is for air to take the supremacy in the three services. We must be predominant in the air at the outset, there will be no time to create new factories or enlarge existing ones.

CHAPTER X

Review

Looking back on those momentous years of the First World War, the years 1916 to 1918, and reviewing them in perspective at a distance of thirty-five years, one seems able to see more clearly the major issues and crises and to be able to weigh the effect of the decisions taken and the course adopted.

At the outset, and during the years in question, we were travelling along unfamiliar and uncharted tracks, full of pitfalls and dangers. It was vital to the future history of our race, and indeed to the world, that we should win the first round, even though at heavy cost. Indeed we made a better start than we deserved in view of our lack of foresight and preparedness, for we were fortunate enough to be able to complete our preparations after the outbreak of war, thanks to the arduous and effective action of the French during the first two years, and eventually to beat our enemy decisively.

Then, faced with new difficulties, many of them of an unfamiliar character and some beyond our control, we forgot the lesson we had learned and reverted to our habitual condition of unpreparedness.

Nevertheless, we had won the war in 1918, and one of the outstanding men who guided our country and our army through those dark and difficult days, in spite of all the obstacles that were constantly placed in his path, was Haig.

In the winter of 1916–17 he found himself in a vortex of international troubles, in a Europe torn by war from end to end, and in a danger soon to be faced owing to the serious condition of his allies, Russia beginning to dissolve in revolution, France suffering from demoralization, and Italy becoming an anxiety.

He was forced to take a leading part in the control, indirectly if not directly, of the whole European theatre of war at this critical time.

Regarding it retrospectively and describing it briefly, I feel that Haig's strategy, dating from May 1916, may be described as covering the following primary objectives:—

First, to keep the French nation in the war, and the French Army in the field, that is, to prevent a separate peace. If he had not used every means in his power to oppose the serious pressure which was applied to him to surrender the initiative and remain inactive, or to dissipate his force in minor theatres, the French would, as we now know, have been attacked and the war would have in all probability been lost.

Second, to free the Belgian coast, and secure the German submarine bases at Ostende and Zeebrugge which constituted a serious threat to our shipping. For this purpose the first step was to gain the watershed between Ypres and Roulers.

Third, to wear the German Army down both physically and morally. He hit that army again and again, watching carefully that the health and morale of his own troops was standing the strain. By taking this action he successfully protected the French against attack and achieved his first object, while reducing the fighting value of his main enemy. This necessarily involved the closest and continuous study of morale of all the combatant armies; and his forecasts and conclusions were proved to be correct by the final results.

Note. The first three objectives mentioned above were all part of the same theme covered by Haig's frequent remark that 'We must wear the enemy down, but at the same time have an objective.' The first of these was, of course, of a secret character, and not for disclosure. The second had lost part of its urgency in the latter half of 1917.

Fourth, to ensure, so far as lay in his power, the requisite concentration of force on a selected front at the decisive time. The battles which ensued in August 1918 and after were designed and carried out with conspicuous skill.

Fifth, to inculcate faith and confidence—faith in victory and the confidence of the men in themselves, in the cause and in their leadership throughout the whole military hierarchy from privates, non-commissioned officers and officers of all ranks to himself, the Commander-in-Chief. We know that the confidence, high spirit and morale which permeated the whole British Army on the 7th August 1918 (the day before the assault) was perfect. 'They had won their battles before they had started.'

This was Haig's strategy. It, in fact, covers all the issues which induced the Germans to give the final verdict, that Haig possessed strategic ability and that in the end he remained 'MASTER OF THE FIELD.'

I must make some reference to our relations with the French nation more especially in connection with the first objective mentioned above. During 1917 protection for the French Army was demanded by and freely given to the French Commander-in-Chief. The first occasion when the British Army requisitioned the help of the French Army was during the *Kaiserschlacht* of March and April 1918, first on the British right and later on the British left. Chapter VII deals with this phase and criticizes the ineffective execution of the scheme for mutual assistance previously agreed upon. These criticisms were verified and regarded as justifiable by the British Commander-in-Chief and his Chief of Staff, Sir Herbert Lawrence. There was no desire to belittle the action of the French, but to state the plain facts as corroborated by the Official Historian.

In his *Short History of World War I*, Sir James Edmonds relates the events day by day and briefly from the opening of the battle on 21st March to its conclusion, including the expression on the 24th of Pétain's intention to fall back and cover Paris, his removal from chief command, and Foch's appointment in his place. The first intervention by the French was on the morning of the 23rd, with one division; between that date and the 27th, eleven more had arrived and others were approaching. On the 26th, Pétain cancelled, on instructions from Foch, his orders of the 24th regarding the covering of Paris, and issued fresh instructions to Fayolle to cover Amiens and keep liaison with Haig. The battlefront had been falling back steadily between the Oise and the Avre, in the general direction of Montdidier.

The French were apparently obeying Pétain's direction to cover Paris.

On the 27th the crisis of the battle was approaching and I would especially mention four events which should be noted.

First, on the 27th the Germans made a bulge 12 miles wide and 10 miles deep in the French front and captured Montdidier, otherwise no success of any importance was made by the Germans on that day.

Second, on the 28th Foch, at 3.15 p.m., informed Haig that the situation at Montdidier was menacing, 'in consequence the first French divisions absorbed before Montdidier cannot extend the French front towards the Somme; the British 5th Army must therefore remain at all costs. It must reorganize where it is.'

Third, on the 28th, early, the Germans with twenty-nine divisions delivered their assault, known as Operation Mars, against eight British divisions about the junction of the 1st and 3rd British Armies in the Arras sector and were heavily repulsed. The enemy recognized failure and this was the turning point of the whole battle.

Fourth, Haig requested Foch on the same day, the 28th, to order the French to take over more of the line to enable him to collect a reserve, or, alternatively, to instruct the French to counter-attack northward of the Oise against the open German flank; he repeated this request on the 30th, and again on 7th April. Foch replied, in excuse, that 'he knew the British could look after themselves, whilst the French required nursing.'

I have referred briefly to the story of these eight days to show that the French intervention was in fact not effective, but I feel that the French divisions were hardly to blame, a number of them having been brought from a distance without their artillery and with only fifty rounds of rifle ammunition per man; it is difficult to see what else they could do but to fall back as the Germans moved forward, they could certainly not counter-attack. Moreover, intervention in a confused and scattered battle is a most difficult operation under the best conditions, still more so as between allies. The fighting began to die down and except for a final attempt to reach Amiens on the 4th–5th

April, which was defeated by Australians, the battle petered out from exhaustion and inanition. But the battle was then in process of shifting to the north to the Lys valley, and the British were about to face the storm again in the second phase of the *Kaiserschlacht*.

Another reason why I have related the above is because my attention has lately been drawn to Weygand's book *Recalled to Service*. On page 151 he quotes Pétain as saying at the Supreme Council Meeting at Briaire on the 11th June 1940, in front of the British Prime Minister, that in March 1918 he had been able to place twenty divisions at once at the disposal of Gough's army and a few days later to send another twenty, making forty in all to set matters right. This, of course, is difficult to follow, but no doubt the Marshal's memory had become defective; nevertheless, a similar fantastic statement is repeated on page 422.

Again, in the second phase of the *Kaiserschlacht* in the Lys valley to the north there were similar difficulties and criticisms of the French. I have discussed with and I have before me letters and a report from General Sir Thomas Marden, who commanded the 6th British Division on the northern flank of the British Army and later on the southern flank. He was next to the French when they lost Mt. Kemmel and Mt. Scherpenberg, and he gives a detailed account. Further, he relates his experiences in the south when the French systematically attacked one hour after the British and after the German flank had already been turned.

Sir Thomas Marden informed me later that in the history of the 6th Division, which he wrote in 1920, he did not refer to these matters as he understood that others had refrained from mentioning them for fear of giving offence or raising controversy, but he did express his views very strongly in 1936 that the facts should be told, and he was supported in that view by General Sir Walter Braithwaite and others.

I do not propose to refer to these matters again, as the subject has already been mentioned in Chapters VII and VIII. I only do so now as there are so many who feel that the French in 1918 had completely recovered from their moral depression, and that gives a quite erroneous impression.

What is right is that we should remember the self-sacrifice of the French and the overstrain imposed on them from August 1914 to April 1917; but it would be equally wrong to ignore the serious losses, trouble and trials created for the British Army during 1917 and 1918 as the direct result of that overstrain.

There is no intention on my part to suggest that the whole French Army was affected by the mutiny of May 1917. The *French Official History* gives—and I have quoted from it in Chapter II—their estimate of the degree and extent of the unrest and moral depression which existed. It is the official French estimate, not mine. I recognize that to generalize from the particular is illogical and unreal; it is equally absurd to assume that because some troops were unreliable, all were unreliable, or vice versa.

CONCENTRATION AT THE DECISIVE POINT

An important feature of the year 1917, after the French defeat on the Aisne, was the repeated pressure brought to bear by the Prime Minister to suspend operations in France and Flanders, and that British troops should be sent from France to support and reinforce an Italian attack on the Austrians. Fortunately the majority of the War Cabinet did not agree to these proposals. The suggestion violated an important axiom of war, namely, that effort and force should be concentrated at the decisive point; this, *per contra*, naturally indicates the corresponding importance of avoiding the dissipation of force on ventures of a secondary character, unrelated directly to the main issue.

France and Flanders constituted the main theatre; it was there that the main German Army was, and where it was likely to remain, still further strengthened by additional divisions released from the Eastern Front; it was also there that protection had to be afforded to the French Army for its preservation. The main issue must inevitably be contested there and to that theatre all possible Allied strength should be directed. There is generally a main theatre and a main issue, and it profits little to knock away minor props in side issues, where those side issues have little bearing on the main issue.

I might refer here to a remark of the Director of Naval Intelligence in Washington, in a book which attracted attention at the time entitled *High Command in the War*, published in 1924. After making the remark, by the way, that 'the great qualities of Haig will become increasingly appreciated by his countrymen,' he adds that 'the dispersal of French and British forces in sideshows nearly brought defeat to the Allies.' The British Army would have found itself wholly in accord with the American view.

BATTLES OF ATTRITION, CASUALTIES AND MORALE

I feel I must say a word about the third and fifth objectives in Haig's strategy as stated by me above. This covers the maintenance of morale, the battles of attrition, the effect of casualties, and faith in victory.

The achievement of these two objectives in the First World War is quite remarkable; I have always felt that there was something about Haig's strong character which infused confidence into the rank and file of the Army, in spite of the fact that he was almost inarticulate. Battles of attrition are unpopular, costly and difficult to justify; the battles of Flanders in 1917 were in fact battles of attrition though their primary object was to draw the enemy's attention away from the French; the prospect of securing the submarine bases in Belgium faded as their importance also faded in the autumn of that year. The casualties were heavy, physical conditions almost unbearable, and prospects of early decision negligible, nevertheless morale remained sound.

In 1918 British and Commonwealth troops went into battle against great odds, and there was no lack of confidence; even in the 5th Army which was overwhelmed and the troops continuously falling back the morale of the men after the third day began to rise while that of the Germans began to fall. I believe that all through 1918 our troops had faith in final victory, whereas the Germans felt that they were fighting a losing war.

Casualties reported are no accurate criterion of the fighting value and effort of the troops involved. Prisoners captured are reckoned as casualties and they include voluntary surrenders.

The consensus of opinion in 1917–18 was that the Germans purposely diminished the numbers reported by about thirty per cent. for reasons of morale on the home front; the French are supposed to have exaggerated theirs by twenty per cent. to prove to the world their effort; the British official figures were not gerrymandered, and were as accurate as possible, but on occasions were twenty per cent. less than those frequently quoted even from authoritative sources, e.g. the authentic battle and wastage British casualties in Flanders 1917 were 238,000, but the number frequently and erroneously quoted was over 400,000.

Whatever hypothetical arguments may be adduced, the clear fact stands out that the British and Commonwealth troops went into battle on the 8th August 1918 on the top of their form with the firm conviction that victory was theirs and in sight.

It would be unfair not to give Haig some substantial credit for this result.

BATTLES

The battles of the First World War were costly to both sides; there were no flanks to turn; they involved frontal attacks and depended for success on the destruction of the enemy by massed artillery fire. Battles were necessary to retain the initiative and prevent the launching of an attack against the French. This was not a war of movement, massed armour, massed air power and carpet bombing. It was a war of thousands of tons of barbed wire, and millions of rounds of artillery ammunition of all calibres; wire to hold up the German infantry and shells to destroy the German wire.

If the Germans had wrested the initiative from the British in 1917 as they might have done and should have done, a very critical situation would no doubt have been created. But their General Staff failed to do the obviously right thing in 1917, as they failed to do on almost every occasion in the First World War from 1914 onwards, and this was of inestimable value to the British. The German task was not the easy one which they experienced in the Franco-Prussian War of 1870, in which the control of the French Army was defective.

The German General Staff may be expert at drafting strategical plans for waging war, but in the execution of their own strategy their judgement seems often to have been halting and faulty.

There were three clear opportunities in the First World War thrown away by the incompetence of the German General Staff.

First, in 1914, during the later development of the great outflanking movement through Belgium, when the occupation of Paris or the Channel ports or both might have been achieved, the German General Staff showed up in a bad light. First, undue optimism gave rise to change of plan, followed by undue pessimism and premature and hasty change of direction and objective. Subsequently confusion reigned. One of Ludendorf's most trusted subordinates, then at German Headquarters, described the scene: 'A panic had seized the leaders; Von Moltke (Chief of the General Staff) sat apathetic, a broken man; Von Stein, his deputy, said "We must not lose our heads," but did nothing.' A case of order, counter-order, and disorder. Hence the battle of the Marne and the German retreat. Von Moltke was sent back to Berlin in consequence of his failure.

Second, in 1917. After the defeat of the French armies on the Aisne in April, the German Crown Prince, in May and June, proposed to deliver an attack across the Aisne opposite Paris to test the condition of the French defences. The *German Official History* states, 'no one could have been more eager to give the order to attack than the High Command, if this had been considered possible, but it was unable to do so.' An estimate had been made that such an attack would require thirty divisions, but only twenty-three were available, and of these 'eight were already on their way to strengthen the Northern Group, in order to meet the British offensive in Flanders which appeared imminent.'

Possibly thirty divisions would have been necessary to reach Paris, but fifteen would have been ample to test the French front and French morale. It was little short of folly that priority should have been given to the reinforcement of the Flanders front, over the necessity to probe the condition of the French Army after its recent defeat. Actually, about this time, the

French War Minister has revealed that only two reliable French divisions stood between Soissons (on the Aisne) and Paris.

Third, in 1918. Between the 24th and 27th March the Germans had almost driven a wedge in between the French and British Armies. The British were fighting stubbornly but the French were giving way. The obvious action for the Germans was to make an immediate and concentrated attack on the French side of the junction point. This the Germans failed to do; instead, on the 28th March, twenty-nine German divisions made a heavy assault on eight British divisions at the junction of the 1st and 3rd British Armies, and were very heavily defeated, gaining no ground. This was regarded afterwards as the real climax of the *Kaiserschlacht*. But what an opportunity missed if some of those twenty-nine German divisions had attacked the French flank near the point of junction with the British.

Battles were necessary, they always are in war; by them Haig retained the initiative, controlled the situation, and was indeed master of the situation.

UNITY OF COMMAND*

I must add one word regarding unity of command. It was agreed at the Doullens conference on the 26th March that unity of command was essential, and Foch was appointed at once to take over direction of operations on the Western Front from that date. Responsibility for the safety of the British Army had not been provided for. A French commander could not take the responsibility, nor could a British commander acting under orders of a Frenchman; nor, obviously, could the British Cabinet take the responsibility for an army in the field. A conference held at Beauvais on the 3rd April settled, so far as it could, the problem by creating the proviso that the commander of either a British, American or French Army had the right of appeal to his Government if, in his opinion, the safety of his army was endangered by any order received from Foch, who was appointed Generalissimo.

* See Chapter VI

There were only four cases in which the right of appeal was suggested, for it was never brought into operation. In the first two, the British Cabinet suggested to Haig that he might wish to appeal, but Haig refused to do so, and accepted full responsibility. In the first case Haig was approached by General Smuts, who had been specially sent for that purpose by the Cabinet. In the second case Haig received a telegram from the Chief of the Imperial General Staff expressing a caution from the Cabinet as to carrying out an order by Foch. In the third and fourth cases Haig objected to Foch's orders and Foch gave way. All these four cases have been related fully in Chapter VIII.

As a matter of fact Haig and Foch worked very well together. By the end of April Foch came to rely on Haig more and more, recognized his ability and consulted him on almost every occasion. They certainly had differences of opinion. Early in September, on the recommendation of Haig, Foch altered the whole strategic direction of his advance from a divergent to a convergent approach, which led to victory.

PREPARATION, ARMAMENT AND THE TWO WORLD WARS

Lack of preparation, or one might almost call it absence of preparation, has been common in all the wars waged by Britain in the last century, including the last two great wars. Providence has indeed been kind to us on each of the last two occasions, when we engaged in war on the continent of Europe on a grand scale. Yet, in both cases, we emerged victorious with enhanced military prestige.

Apart from the absence of preparation and the troubles experienced with the French Army in both wars, there was little or no similarity between the two wars.

The first war lasted for four and a quarter years; its character was almost entirely static; it covered an area wider than ever before, extending from the Caucasus to the Atlantic, and from the Baltic to the Mediterranean. Science with invention were just beginning to impinge on warfare. The aeroplane and tank were developing but were in an experimental stage and not yet in requisite supply. The submarine was playing an important part. Massed artillery of all calibres constituted the main offensive weapon. America entered the war with the arrival of an increasing number of divisions during the last few months.

The second war lasted for five and three-quarter years. Its character was almost entirely dynamic, with large-scale amphibious operations. After a bad start with the twilight war and the surrender of France, Britain made a wonderful recovery. A much larger area was covered by the war than on the previous occasion, stretching east and west all round the earth, and from the Arctic Ocean to the Southern Seas. The Air Force took its place alongside the Army and Navy in battle, in reconnaissance, in bombing, and its importance grew rapidly until it dominated by land, sea and air not only the battle area but all communications and the home area. Tanks and armour generally became rapidly indispensable to offensive operations. Science had made great strides between the two world wars from radar to rockets and to atom bombs. The Americans entered the war effectively with large forces well equipped, efficient and determined. Russia played an important part in the east, being rolled back by Germany to the Volga, and rolling forward again to enter Germany. Germany and Japan were tough adversaries, but the might of Britain, America and Russia was decisive.

After the First World War, our financial and economic condition showed signs of wear and tear. The large increase in the National Debt, the high level of taxation, the liquidation of overseas assets, the falling off of invisible exports, the slender margin in balance of payments, the repudiation of our debt to America, and many other features all gave cause for thought of the future; and many did think deeply as to the ways and means of meeting the requirements of a possible second war. Such thoughts, together with increasing pressure for restraint in expenditure and general economy, were no doubt partly the cause of procrastination in our defensive preparations for the second war, in spite of the bullying behaviour of Germany and the threatening atmosphere.

Nor was the economic outlook promising; the home country could do no more than feed two-thirds of its population; the temper of those engaged in industry and agriculture did not appear to encourage the prospect of increasing production and enlarging our export market.

Those who expressed anxiety at the time soon found, as the second war developed, covering a greater area and a longer period, all at greater cost, that they had not overstated their case. On the conclusion of peace in 1945, the country emerged in a condition not far removed from bankruptcy.

Meanwhile, we must press forward with rearmament, curb inflation by more drastic means, and tighten our belts. The one encouraging feature is that the Western democracies are preparing, and taking rearmament seriously, thus making war less probable.

But the Turn of History seems still to be on the march, even increasing its pace and widening its scope under the threat of war from the communist countries of the world.

COMMANDER-IN-CHIEF

'Nations have not infrequently been led astray by the influence of theories propounded, either for the sake of originality, or the advertisement they bring.' I cannot locate the author of this quotation, and should he happen to see it here, I offer him my apology for using it.

There is importance, however, in this statement, especially in relation to wars in which suffering through loss and hardship had been severe; there are opportunities for showing originality and acquiring advertisement, but incidentally obscuring reality and truth.

In this book I neither claim originality nor do I desire advertisement; nevertheless, I trust that readers of these pages may be influenced by what I have, with some knowledge and much sincerity, written.

Field-Marshal Lord Haig remarked to me on many occasions when talking of those years, 1917 and 1918, and of the ignorance of fact and suppression of truth which were so common, that we must exercise patience, await publication of the Official Histories, and a more distant perspective in the future, free from bias, to see the truth laid bare. The Official Histories have now been published, and the present is now the future to which Lord Haig alluded. The heat of controversy at the time should now give way to cool judgement and a proper perspective of the debt we owe to him.

This seems to be the appropriate moment to study his task and its completion, to pay tribute to a great Captain, and to the man who remained:

'MASTER OF THE FIELD'

He fulfilled his task with tenacity, consummate skill and complete success, in the face of almost insurmountable difficulties, and in spite of the fact that, for a long period, Britain was fighting alone.

He met every crisis with careful forethought, calculated prevision and sound judgement.

He gave his allies all the help he could, to tide them over their difficulties and their misfortunes.

Four victories crushed the German Army: Broodseinde on the 4th October 1917; the *Kaiserschlacht* on the 21st March 1918; Amiens on the 8th August 1918; and the Hindenburg Line on the 27th September 1918. They were all British and Commonwealth victories, won under his leadership.

He conducted the final series of battles to victory with masterly proficiency. The strategy was his strategy, adopted by Foch in preference to his own.

He maintained the high prestige of the British Nation and Army throughout the war.

He kept the respect and confidence of the men who fought under him and he preserved their splendid morale.

He served his country well, and never for a moment, up to the day of his death, did he forget the welfare of the men who had fought under his command; nor has the British Legion forgotten him.

THE BENT SWORD

by A. M. G.

(with kind permission of its Author)

AN ARTICLE FROM BLACKWOOD'S MAGAZINE, JANUARY 1944

THERE is an episode, direful in its possibilities, of the First World War which even now is veiled in mystery. For a curtain of silence, almost impenetrable, despite the passing of a quarter of a century, hides the great mutinies in the French Armies in 1917. The stern necessities of that black year naturally enforced the utmost reticence on all, even within the charmed circle of the High Command. But the curious feature of the whole lamentable episode is that the veil has never been pierced by the patient researches of innumerable military historians. Here and there a corner has been lifted, but only a glimpse of the drama has been caught by an interested world. In these circumstances it seems presumptuous that I, a mere amateur, should offer to conduct 'Maga's' readers behind the scenes. But chance, in the shape of a discovery in a little-used library, has given me a clearer insight into the drama of the mutinies which bade fair to wreck the Allied cause in 1917. And so, with that apologia, we shall, like David Balfour, plunge *in medias res*.

The literature is scanty. The German General Staff, with Teutonic thoroughness, has prepared two slim monographs on the collapse of French morale. I have read them, and am struck by the note of chagrin which underlies the stiff phrases of the bemedalled author. For, thanks to the reticence aforementioned, Von Hindenburg and his *alter ego* Ludendorff, remained in blissful ignorance of the fact that the whole Western Front was in their grasp. Happily, when the news trickled through to Spa, via Switzerland, it was too late to do anything. And the dissolution of the Imperial Germany was by that failure of military Intelligence made an absolute certainty. Which is a lesson to us today on the dangers of careless talk.

The French, most naturally, have contributed little to the penetration of the curtain. A few articles have appeared in technical journals, but they are almost valueless as dispassionate judgments. For one and all insist that the High Command at Chantilly was not to blame for the failure of morale, and vehemently make the civil Government the scapegoat for the débâcle. On that the reader must judge for himself.

Two or three authors, mostly of the extreme Left, have, with equal sound and fury, impeached the General Staff. So from a dazzling mist of words only one fact emerges. And that is that the mutinies were vast, deadly dangerous, and a lesson to the statesman and soldier that poor humanity has its limitations.

Mutinies, indeed, occurred in the forces of all the belligerents of 1914–18. Some were sporadic and quickly suppressed. Others like that of the High Seas Fleet paved the way to revolution. Even in easy-going Britain the fighting men showed their teeth, but, as is the British way, not until the main job was done. But the French collapse threatened the very existence of the Allies at a time when they were fighting for their lives. Perhaps the tragedy of June 1940 cast its shadow before in a black summer twenty-three years earlier.

For France has been sick for a long time. An officer of the Fighting French, intelligent like all his race, once told me that he believed his country had never bridged the bloody chasm of the Terror of 1792, when a nation went mad and the guillotine rose and fell in ghastly rhythm. Even the incomparable victories of the Emperor have now a curiously ephemeral quality. The tinsel Second Empire of his nephew lacked the solidity of a united nation, and in the red ruin of Sedan its nakedness was discovered to an amazed world. The Third Republic, born in the days of disaster, rocked perilously as General Boulanger and Captain Dreyfus played their destined parts, and below the placid surface of France strange ferments of anarchy, pacifism, defeatism, and even treason were at work as the twentieth century opened.

A conscript army is the mirror of the civil population from which it is drawn, and the French Army was no exception. The growing industrialisation of the country had encouraged the rise of a turbulent, class-conscious mass of workers, and to the natural individuality of the Frenchman was added the catalyst of radical ideas. The fiery oratory of Jaurès and the rising revolutionary lawyer, Pierre Laval, had set strange currents of internationalism stirring in the veins of the conscript drafts which annually were called to the Colours. The seeds of 1917 were being sown as Europe fumbled uneasily through the first decade of the century.

In Paris the Olympians of the Supreme War Council were not unaware of the trend of affairs. But as the German menace loomed ever nearer with each successive crisis, they had other things to cogitate. In sharp reaction to the counsels of timidity, founded on the débâcle of 1870, came the doctrine of the offensive. No longer, preached the brilliant Colonel Foch, must France be passive behind the frontier fortifications of the gifted engineer Séré de Riviére. She must use the great forts as spring-boards to launch an irresistible attack on the field-grey plodding legions. And in April 1914 the seal of official approval was given to the dazzling tactics of the attack. For good or ill, the High Command had decided on "l'attaque à outrance."

A thousand miles to the south-east a shot rang out on a June day in Sarajevo. The hatreds of a continent boiled over as Slav and Teuton manœuvred for position. And as the drums ruffled the proclamation of

'Kriegsgefahrzustand' (state of danger of war) in Berlin, anxious Ministers and their official subordinates met in Paris.

It was a high matter of State which they had to discuss that hot August afternoon. No less, in fact, than the use to which a fat folio should be put. Carnet 'B' the high officials of the Interior called it, and in it were the names of 2,501 Frenchmen who were to be arrested on general mobilisation. Among them was that rising politician of the Left, M. Pierre Laval. He and his colleagues were, in the opinion of the Government, of so deleterious an influence on national morale that their immediate incarceration was advisable. M. Laval, the intelligent reader will observe, has run true to form for nearly thirty years.

There was high debate that afternoon of long ago. The Ministers, alarmed by the reports of the Prefects, were disinclined for drastic action lest the workers, bereft of their chosen leaders, should rise. In their quandary they turned to the old Tiger, M. Georges Clemenceau, for advice. It was, as might be expected, that the wholesale arrests should take place at once, and with it the Prefect of the Police agreed. But a calmer voice sounded when the Chief of the Sûreté was consulted. 'The workers,' he said, 'will not rise. They will follow the regimental bands.'

He was right. A crowded Chamber passed the decree of General Mobilisation with acclamation, and overnight the posters calling up the 'Armies of the Land and Sea' appeared on the walls of every town hall. In their thousands the reservists flocked to the colours, and M. Laval and his confrères remained mute and unmolested. Thus in the face of deadly peril France closed her ranks. There were no longer masters and servants, exploiters and workers; only Frenchmen. Guided by Plan XVII and the strategy of the offensive, the armies of France plunged into war.

Sixty-five divisions she mobilised. And of that vast army only 509 soldiers deserted during the terrible winter of 1914. Morale was very high in those days.

The bloody years rolled on. In Chantilly deferential staff officers placed the mounting toll of death before that national nerve sedative, General Joffre. A quarter million, a half million—still the total mounted as France bled herself white in the shambles of Verdun. Three hundred thousand Frenchmen died to hold that dismantled Fortress, and still the offensive doctrine held lordship of the ascendant. Through the crash of the barrage and the swish of lead, besnouted figures clambered out of water-logged trenches to dash themselves in red ruin on a stubborn enemy. The soldier, as one of them said, was being too much tried.

There were other factors which contributed to the general slackening of morale as 1916 drew to its close.

The soldiers' pay, miserable in peace, was ridiculously inadequate at a time when civilian rewards were swollen beyond the bounds of the thrifty French mind. The fighting man saw, with increasing bitterness, his wife and children queue up for a pittance, while fat profiteers and aliens wallowed in the incredible wages and profits of war. His food was scanty and monotonous, his drink vile and sometimes poisonous. In the brief spells of rest out of the line he would sleep in a draughty barn or filthy cowshed. Amenities, such as those provided for his Allies by the Y.M.C.A., were unknown, or, at the best, hopelessly inadequate and tainted by conscious charity. But greatest of all grievances was that of leave.

It was scanty and irregular in the highest degree. The persistent offensives had time and again caused all leave to be cancelled at short notice, and there were cases recorded of men having had none for thirty months. Even when it was granted, it was rarely pleasurable. There was the long comfortless journey home in broken-windowed and crowded carriages, and the perpetual chivying of railway transport officers and gendarmes, ever on the alert for the deserter. Once home, there was little for a man with a few francs in his pocket to do in a world of incredible prices and opulent civilians. So it is not surprising that the insidious words and pamphlets of the subversive agitator found good soil in the front-line soldier on leave. Then there would be the long trek back, when a glum man had time to think of his miserable lot. That he should resist the temptation to grumble to his comrades is too much to expect of hard-driven humanity. And with the sodden spring of 1917, the rot spread in the armies of France.

Of these tendencies the High Command was not ignorant. Secret Service men, euphemistically named observers, mingled with the fighting troops, and their reports on morale grew more and more pessimistic as the weeks went by. Trained censors scrutinised the soldiers' mail, and their findings dovetailed accurately with those of the Secret Service. Thousands of pamphlets, treasonably defeatist in tone, were flooding into the front line and rear of the Armies, and the response of their recipients showed that something was very rotten in the State. Like their British forerunners in the Revolutionary Wars, the French High Command had reason to be apprehensive of the power of the printed and spoken word on the soldier—

> 'Come, little drummer boy,
> Lay down your knapsack here.
> I am the soldiers' friend.
> Here are some books for you.
> Nice clever books by Tom
> Paine the philanthropist.'

But unlike the men of the Scots Guards who offered £200 reward for the apprehension of the agitator who sought to subvert their loyalty in 1797, the French Armies of 1917 were in no condition to resist the voice of the tempter.

April 1917. General Nivelle, the paladin of Verdun, had assumed command, and, *non sine pulvere*, had obtained the reluctant consent of his Government for one last decisive offensive. Like wildfire, the news spread amongst the war-weary troops that at long length the final blow was to be struck, and that by the summer they would be back in their homes. Behind the lines vast numbers of guns, ammunition and stores were accumulated, and night and day the mud-sodden roads carried a myriad of transport. Close to the front the cavalry assembled in readiness to exploit the inevitable break-through. And in the fighting men a high desperate gallantry flared up, perhaps for the last time.

Far to the rear the Commander-in-Chief, free at last from vexatious civilian interference, bent over the vast maps and, satisfied, straightened his soldierly figure. At his elbow the brilliant consumptive, Colonel d'Alenson, stood ready with the final operation orders. Moulded by his clear brain, they were models of mathematical precision in their way, but bearing the dread stigmata of *'spes phthisica'* in their avoidance of unpleasant essentials. For the neglected medical services were studiously ignored, and the question of air support for the advance was left to be solved by the famed 'Systeme D' on the spot.

Incredibly, in bland disregard of the German command of the air, Nivelle has nothing to say to the frantic representations of his subordinate commanders. It was a grim omen of 1940.

The sleet, driven by a bitter wind, blattered against the windows of G.Q.G. that April night. In the trenches the freezing shower beat down pitilessly on the curved drenched backs of the waiting soldiers. Beside them the black Senegalese, France's colonial children, crouched in a frozen apathy. Overhead thousands of shells screamed and rumbled as the barrage worked up to its maximum. In the rear the sky blazed, and the earth rocked as the gunners increased their rate of fire. Then with shattering suddenness the rain of steel ceased, and at first light of 16th April 1917 the infantry attacked. The final battle had been joined.

As the morning wore on, hope in Grand Quartier General faded. Outside the rain poured down in torrents, and the ground over which the advance had to be made, already shell torn, was a quagmire. In the Third Bureau the Chief of Operations professed to a complete lack of news, and the evening communiqué was vague and uninformative. Stress was laid on the enemy resistance and the difficulties of the terrain. It is not thus that a Commander paves the way to the announcement of victories.

By the 19th the momentum, such as it was, of the offensive was spent. At the cost of 120,000 casualties a certain amount of ground had been gained and 20,000 prisoners taken. But it was not those petty prizes that the armies had been promised. It was another Ulm or Austerlitz, a complete annihilating victory of the Napoleonic type. And when that eluded their desperate grasp something died in their hearts. It was the end of a dream, of the will to fight, of Frenchmen. For France, not for the last time, had been, through her muzzled Press and Parliament, too much lied to.

Nivelle's star set a few days later. A Napoleon devoid of genius, he trailed miserably with his entourage to Senlis, the Stellenbosch of the French Army. And General Philippe Pétain reigned in his stead.

In grim anticipation of 1940, he entered into an unhappy heritage. For the cancer of defeatism was eating into the armies of France, and the rot was widespread when the hero of Verdun grasped the reins of command. And not for the first time nor the last, the sinister figure of M. Malvy, Radical politician and Minister of the Interior, comes on to the stage of European history.

This gentleman had, in the course of a somewhat circuitous career, acquired those desirable things, money and power. Beginning as a firebrand of the most lurid type, he was looked upon by the Trades Unions as a barrier to reaction. Be that as it may, M. Malvy, Minister of the Interior of the French Republic, had some very queer friends. Uncharitable persons, doubtless jealous of the good man's rise, went so far as to whisper that M. Malvy's private life was of such an interesting nature that the attention of the German Secret Service had been called to it. At any rate, the Minister seemed well supplied with this world's goods, and it is possible that Berlin occasionally gave him tokens of esteem—in return, of course, for a few trifling favours which M. Malvy in his official position had no difficulty in performing. So, at least, ran the whisper through the strange underworld of the 'Republic of Pals.' Certainly M. Clemenceau in his *L'Homme Libre* never ceased to inveigh against the Minister and his friends over the Rhine. And the Tiger was no mean judge of men.

But, to the satisfaction of himself and his supporters, M. Malvy was able to muzzle the Tiger, and soon a startled public saw the long blacked-out columns of *L'Homme Libre*, now renamed *L'Homme Enchaîné*, which had received the censor's attention. M. Malvy was, we must admit, a gentleman of ability and determination. He and his friends of the 'Bonnet Rouge,' that secret society of German-subsidised traitors, knew when they were well off.

There were, however, keen eyes watching his dazzling progress to the heights of French politics. M. Gaston Bruyant and Lieutenant Jacques Duval of the Bureau of Morale had noted that M. Malvy was strangely uninterested in the steady rise of defeatist propaganda in the Army. Indeed M. Bruyant so far forgot the respect due to a Minister as to tell him to his face that he ought to be under lock and key. But M. Malvy was used to calumny and treated the insubordination with that gracious, not to say oily, nonchalance which had made him the darling of certain Paris salons and their fair, frail occupants. And the stream of defeatist propaganda became a flood as embittered men pondered over the failure of the great offensive. In May 1917 the Secret Service reports to G.Q.G. rose to a pitch of almost hysterical warning. And soon their authors had the melancholy satisfaction of being proved Cassandras of the most accurate type.

The first rumblings of the storm inevitably came from the effervescent capital. On May Day a 'Committee for the Renewal of International Relations' brought 15,000 citizens to a demonstration. And of that number a fair portion came from the fighting men. Despite a police ban, the meeting was held in the Place de la République, and resolutions of a highly defeatist nature were carried with acclamation. Leaflets of a most subversive and seditious type were scattered broadcast amongst the crowds, and a good number returned to the front in the pockets of disgruntled soldiers. It is perhaps superfluous to add that the high-souled members of the Committee were under certain pecuniary obligations to guttural-spoken gentlemen and (not so guttural) ladies in Switzerland. The Fifth Column, you see, is not a new development, particularly in unhappy France.

The fuse thus fired travelled briskly to the powder magazine. On 3rd May it blew up with shattering intensity when the 21st Division of Colonial Infantry refused duty as one man. The General, however, long used to truculent soldiery, acted with decision, and within a few hours the ring-leaders were under close arrest and their dupes back to their obedience. Two days later the division went into action, where it acquitted itself with credit, though at terrible cost. The agitators were then court-martialled and sentenced to long periods of exile in dread Cayenne.

So far, so good. G.Q.G. were informed of the mutiny, but apparently considered that the Divisional Commander's promptitude had scotched the snake. At all events, nothing was done except the circulation of a secret order enjoining vigilance on the part of all senior officers.

The Olympian calm, however, was of short duration. On the 19th May the 120th Regiment of Infantry refused to leave their rest billets and move up the line. An attempt was made to arrest the leaders of the revolt, but failed dismally. The loyal N.C.O.s and men were surrounded by the mutineers, insulted, and disarmed. Then the regiment rested from its labours and indulged in a spate of defeatist oratory which lasted until the early hours of the 20th.

Meanwhile a frantic Colonel had seen his General, and orders from Divisional H.Q. directed that the 128th Regiment should shame the mutineers by taking their place in the firing line. But the issue of orders and their execution are two very different matters, and the men of the 128th were disinclined for the rôle of shining example. On the morning of the 21st they made contact with the 120th, and the two regiments barricaded themselves in their billets and improvised fortifications. To the pleas of their officers one answer was returned, 'We'll never enter the trenches again.'

For four days the mutineers waited. Then food ran short, and they quietly surrendered. Three soldiers were shot, and the remainder dispersed to other units. There, by some incredible mistake, they were allowed to mix freely with their new comrades, most of whom were ripe for mutiny.

The hurricane, though strong, had not yet reached its full intensity. During the last two weeks in May sporadic disturbances broke out in widely scattered formations, but they were quickly put down, and it was not till the first days of June that the storm broke in deadly earnest.

On the 2nd of that month two battalions mutinied at Soissons. A committee of delegates was appointed on the model of the 1797 mutinies at

145

Spithead, and a series of conditions for return to duty drawn up. They included an immediate hundred per cent increase in pay, regular leave, better dependants' allowances, improved food, and, most significant of all, an assurance that no further offensive should be undertaken unless the enemy's wire and trenches were completely shattered by artillery preparation. Finally, an amnesty clause guaranteed the freedom from punishment for the participants in the mutiny.

To these demands G.Q.G. and the Government could only return a firm negative, and the mutineers proceeded to march on Paris to enforce their will on Parliament. Loyal coloured troops were hastily rushed up from the south, and some bitter fighting took place at the railway stations and road junctions. Over eighty men were bayoneted or shot one bloody afternoon.

Farther to the east a regiment marched docilely enough to the front, but persisted in 'baaing' to indicate they were sheep led to the slaughter. To their officers' remonstrances came a swift reply. The regimental transport was seized, and, laden with mutineers waving red flags, turned back to the rest billets from which they came.

All along the French sectors there were violent manifestations of revolt. The 119th Artillery Regiment mounted machine-guns on their lorries and attempted to reach the great munition works of Schneider-Creusot. A General, bravely attempting to recall his men to their duty by personal intervention, was violently beaten and insulted. Innumerable lesser officers found themselves stripped of all authority, though in most cases they were treated with respect. And all the time a steady stream of deserters trickled to the rear. In the summer of 1917 no less than 21,174 desertions were reported.

In Paris, consternation reigned. Large numbers of Senegalese troops were rushed in to garrison the capital against the mutineers who, the Cabinet believed, were marching on the city. The imperturbable M. Malvy, however, appeared to view the situation with creditable calm, and only exerted his powers against his traducers by a tightening of the censorship. Strangely enough, however, he was hoist with his own petard. For unintelligent subordinates applied the iron grasp of suppression on all the frontiers, including the Swiss. And certain gentlemen who wished to make a voyage found themselves with much to explain to the Security Control Officers. There were, after all, keen brains and loyal hearts in the France of 1917. That they remain we do not doubt.

For a fortnight that unhappy June, matters went from bad to worse at the front. Unit after unit refused duty, and where officers were unwise enough to offer violence, blood was shed. At the peak of the mutinies no less than sixteen army corps were affected in a greater or lesser degree. According to M. Painlevé, the Minister for War, in his report to the Chamber, only two divisions out of twelve on the Champagne sector were loyal. At other places the trenches were scarcely manned. No wonder the German monographs on the mutinies betray the chagrin of the Oberkommando!

The new Commander-in-Chief had a hard row to hoe, and whatever his subsequent record, we must admit that Pétain bent to his task with loyal goodwill. From a reluctant Government, jealous of military usurpation, he obtained the power to inflict the death penalty without reference to Paris, as had formerly been the case. Courts martial rapidly constituted were enjoined to the utmost severity. But at the same time the Commander-in-Chief slipped the velvet glove over the iron hand. By personal visits, by promises, by appeals to the honour and patriotism of his troops, he gradually reduced the fever to manageable point. Certain high officers were removed, and others promoted in their stead. By careful nursing, Pétain raised the morale of his men till they were convalescent and able to undertake a most successful little offensive. He was, in those happy days, the physician of a sick Army.

The fate of the ringleaders of the mutiny is obscure. One hundred and fifty-seven death sentences were passed, but only twenty-three men were shot. There is, however, some reason to believe that particularly mutinous formations were deliberately sent to dangerous fronts, and Henri Barbusse goes so far as to affirm that 250 mutineers were marched to a quiet sector and annihilated by French shells. There are many dark places still in the story of those June days when the Allied cause trembled in the balance.

Of the good M. Malvy there is little more to relate. One unhappy day for him, the implacable Clemenceau became for all practical purposes Dictator, and M. Malvy saw the inside of a prison cell. Fortified, doubtless, by his conscious integrity he faced the charge of treason before the Senate, sitting as a high court, with his customary calm. But after a display of forensic fireworks and much mud-slinging, all in the highest traditions of Gallic jurisprudence, M. Malvy was convicted on a lesser charge, that of malfeasance while in office. To the layman his sentence of five years' banishment seems a little inadequate.

His equivocal friends of the Bonnet Rouge were not so fortunate. Almeyreda died in mysterious circumstances in his prison cell. Suicide, said the Government. Murder, said that indefatigable Royalist, M. Daudet. A lady of sinuous charms, Mata Hari, was shot, as was Bolo Pasha. But these unfortunates had not been Cabinet Ministers. They had not, therefore, had an opportunity to learn too much. M. Malvy was, however, in that happy position, and lived to stage a glorious comeback in the Augean stable of French politics. The Trade Unions did not desert their paladin.

In 1917 the sword of France was bent. In 1940 it was broken. But, tempered by the fires of war and defeat, it will, as her friends know, shine once again in the armoury of a cleaner world.

PREFACE

TO THE

BRITISH OFFICIAL HISTORY

MILITARY OPERATIONS FRANCE AND BELGIUM, VOL II 1917
7TH JUNE TO 10TH NOVEMBER

Reproduced by kind permission of its Author

Brigadier-General Sir James Edmonds, CB, CMG, RE,
HON.D.LITT(OXON)
and with the authority of The Controller, H.M. Stationery Office

THIS volume contains the account of the two Flanders offensives of 1917 called, officially, 'The Battle of Messines 1917' (7th–14th June), and 'The Battles of Ypres 1917' (31st July–10th November)—the latter better known as 'Third Ypres' or even as 'Passchendaele.'

The Battle of Messines, with its tremendous artillery bombardment and its record explosion of land mines containing nearly a million pounds of high explosive, was a triumph of organization and of the co-operation of the artillery and the engineers with the infantry; it was one of the very few operations of the war in which the infantry, without tanks, had scarcely more to do than go forward and take possession. The only controversial point about 'Messines' is whether, to avoid the heavy casualties which ensued, the infantry should not have gone farther, or whether the main line gained should not have been withdrawn to the reverse slope of the ridge.

With the long-drawn-out fighting before Ypres it is very different. Almost every point in connection with it became in the after years a matter of controversy, or rather a reason for attacking the reputation of Field-Marshal Earl Haig. Its inception, its execution, its continuance, and the ground conditions all came under public review. The campaign was adjudged by (at the time) influential civilian critics as 'purposeless,' 'a reckless gamble . . . with nothing to show but a ghastly casualty list,' 'a muddy and muddle-headed adventure.' Most extraordinary legends obtained circulation and gained general credence. To distort the picture, the name of 'Passchendaele,' that of part, and the bad part of the battle, which rightly belongs only to the last period of four weeks after the weather had broken and conditions did become appalling, has been attached to the whole three and a half months which the Third Battle of Ypres lasted. Thus 'Passchendaele' came to connote not, as it should, a wonderful Canadian success in mud and rain, but a long persistent struggle under such conditions. Essential facts were entirely overlooked: e.g., that September 1917 was a month of fine weather, that several attacks were made in clouds of dust—once through 'a wall of dust and smoke'—and that the ground was so hard as late as the morning of the 4th October that pieces of shell and bullets ricochetted. Ignored, too, were the very good reasons, secret at the time, for attacking in Flanders and continuing to attack in spite of adverse conditions. These reasons were the urgent demands of General Pétain for a diversion on account of the mutinies which had spread through a large part of the French Army, and the demands of the British Admiralty, in consequence of huge shipping losses, for the suppression of the U-boat bases on the Flemish coast. The Intelligence reports of the very serious enemy casualties and the lasting effect of the campaign on his plans and on the morale of his troops and of his Homeland, now known to be correct, were labelled 'extravagant' and 'ridiculous.'

Aspersions on the military character of Field-Marshal Earl Haig should not require contradiction, and the minimizing, even complete ignoring, of the success of his troops, both British and Dominion, should not require correction; but some refutation of the legend cannot be entirely neglected. The mis-statements continue to flourish. They crystallize in what was written in a newspaper article on Earl Haig, eighteen years after events.[1]

> 'Why has not Haig been recognized as one of England's greatest generals? Why, as a national figure, did he count far less than Lord Roberts, whose wars were picnics by comparison? The answer may be given in one word—"Passchendaele".'

Our late enemy thought differently. The following truly represents German military opinion.[2]

> 'The circumstance that Haig never could act really independently, but always had to make his decisions subject to conditions imposed on him, is no reason to deny him the position of a commander-in-chief. Dependence on others was often the fate of great commanders. What is more important is whether his actions were conducted with strategic ability, firm will, strength of character, acceptance of responsibility and political insight. Haig possessed all these qualities and used them in "harmonious combination" as Clausewitz requires of a great commander. By means of these powers he saved France in 1916 and 1917, and pre-eminently on that historic day, the 26th March 1918.[3] Finally:

---

[1] *News Chronicle* of 25th March 1935.

[2] Translated from 'Heerführer des Weltkrieges (Great Commanders of the World War),' issued by the 'Deutsche Gesellschaft für Wehrpolitik und Wehrwissenschaften,' the equivalent of our Royal United Service Institution. It contains excellent appreciations of ten great commanders of 1914–18 by different hands. The selected ten are the younger Moltke, Joffre, Falkenhayn, Conrad, Alexeiev, Enver, Cadorna, Haig, Foch and Hindenburg-Ludendorf. The Grand Duke Nicholas, Maréchal Pétain and General Diaz are not included and neither Sir John French nor Nivelle.

[3] This must refer to the Doullens Conference, when at Haig's suggestion Foch was appointed to co-ordinate the operations—and make Pétain fight.

if the ultimate victory over the Central Powers was not accomplished on the battlefield, but was gained on quite another plane, yet in the last three years of the war Haig contributed the most to prevent a German victory. Thus he really remained "master of the field".'

The reputation of Earl Haig has undoubtedly suffered in England and Wales from the label 'Passchendaele' being attached to him—to connote unnecessary suffering and all the horrors of winter warfare—but it stands high not only in Germany, but in France and in the U.S.A.

The principal items in the indictment against Earl Haig in legend depend on gross exaggeration of the British casualties and on the misrepresentation that the whole area of the battlefield was a morass, ignoring that really muddy conditions were confined to certain stretches and patches, and that the really bad weather extended only over the first and last periods.

As the charges have been made publicly by no less a personage than the Prime Minister at the time, the late Earl Lloyd George, they cannot be overlooked here. The statement, made by him and other eminent writers, which colours the whole of the indictment of Haig is the easiest disproved. It is that the casualties at 'Passchendaele' were 'gigantic,' 'nearly 400,000,' 'more than at the Somme'. The source of this total appears to be the German wireless; it is found in the Bavarian Official Account: 'An 400,000 Mann hatte der Feind auf den Schlachtfeldern Flanders verloren (the enemy had lost about 400,000 men on the battlefields of Flanders).' The statement laid in February 1919 before the Versailles Supreme War Council, when every endeavour was made to make the total as large as possible, gave it as 244,897, including the normal wastage on the Ypres front. The 'Total Battle and Trench Wastage by weeks 31st July–10th November 1917,' compiled at the time by Armies, comes to 238,313. These are contemporary figures, not 'an elaborate effort to gerrymander the casualty returns.'

The battlefield, it was said, was 'a reclaimed swamp, which was only prevented returning to its original condition of a soggy morass by an elaborate system of drainage.' A glance at Map I will show that the scene of the struggle is the ridge on the eastern side of Ypres and the gentle slope leading up to it from the Yser canal; it has never been a morass, except, perhaps, in Mesozoic times, and was drained by its natural slope and a number of small streams. The words quoted above apply to a district called 'les Moeres,' twenty miles away, near the coast between Furnes and Dunkirk.

The Commander-in-Chief has been blamed for defying the bad weather. It is simply not true that, as asserted, 'Flanders was the wettest area on the front,' and that 'in Flanders the weather broke early each August with the regularity of an Indian monsoon'—the weather there is, of course, as variable as on the English south coast. It was not the fault of Sir Douglas Haig that the Flanders campaign was begun so late in the year and thus towards the end encountered the normal October bad weather. He wished to open the operations in March or April, but was prevented from doing so by the

French General Nivelle insisting that the British spring offensive should be staged at Arras, nearer to his own Aisne attack.

It is not, as asserted, the case that 'both British ministers and French generals were strongly opposed to the undertaking,' and that 'the leading French generals had done their best to dissuade us, and had stated emphatically that they condemned the project and thought it a foolish venture which must fail.' It was the exact contrary as regards the French: General Nivelle, when Commander-in-Chief, as early as 21st December 1916, wrote to Sir Douglas Haig: 'If our grand offensive succeeds it is certain that the Belgian coast will fall into our hands as a result of the retreat of the German Armies and without a direct attack. If our attacks fail, it will still be possible to carry out in fine weather the operations projected in Flanders.' When the grand offensive did fail, General Pétain, Nivelle's successor, first proposed to co-operate on the left of the British with twelve divisions, and after the mutinies in the French Army arose begged for the Flanders operation, and volunteered to co-operate in it with the French First Army of six divisions. The French Official History actually states that on the 30th June 1917, when General Anthoine, commander of the French First Army, visited Sir Douglas Haig, he brought a message from General Pétain: 'l'offensive des Flandres doit etre assurée d'un succès absolu, *"impérieusement exigé par les facteurs moraux du moment"*.' (Italicized in original.)

As regards British ministers, the decision to make the main British effort of 1917 in Flanders had been approved by the War Committee of the Cabinet on the 26th October 1916, confirmed on the 23rd November by Mr. Asquith, the Prime Minister, who himself handed personally to Sir Douglas Haig a letter of approval, a copy being sent to the C.I.G.S. An offensive, leaving place and time to the generals—it was well known the place would be Flanders—was sanctioned by the Paris Conference of British and French ministers on 4th–5th May 1917. The situation was obviously changed when the Nivelle offensive had definitely failed and the French Army was declared incapable for a time of further effort. The War Cabinet then had doubts about persisting in the Flanders campaign, even after Messines Ridge had been captured. There were, however, three urgent reasons for the continuance of the campaign (that there was no alternative place is shown in Chapter XIX). First, General Pétain revealed to Sir Douglas Haig, as a military secret, the mutinous state of the French Army and implored him, and continued to implore him, to attack in order to prevent the Germans from taking advantage of this state. Secondly, in consequence of the terrible losses from U-boat attacks (694 merchant ships in the first six months of 1917, amounting to over two million tons), Admiral Jellicoe, the First Sea Lord, stated to the War Cabinet that 'if the army cannot get the Belgian ports, the navy cannot hold the Channel and the War is lost. . . . It is no good making plans for next year.' The third reason was the rapid deterioration of the situation on the Russian front.

Sir Douglas Haig was confident of success. The War Cabinet, unwilling to overrule both naval and military authorities, and officially ignorant of the French mutinies, on 20th July sanctioned the Flanders campaign on the understanding that it would be called off if progress did not reach expectations. A change of attitude more favourable to the offensive then took place probably owing to news of the French mutinies reaching them; for on the 25th July, the War Cabinet, by telegram, assured Sir Douglas Haig of their approval of his plans, and their 'wholehearted support.'

At the end of August the Prime Minister at a War Cabinet meeting spoke about closing down the Flanders campaign, and in order to gain his own way he even contemplated a change of commander-in-chief if a suitable successor could be found. He called in for professional advice, not his constitutional advisers, but two officers, Field-Marshal Lord French and Lieutenant-General Sir Henry Wilson, bitter enemies of Sir Douglas Haig, and they both supported his views.[1] Later the Prime Minister received some backing from Mr Winston Churchill, the Minister of Munitions, who though sparing no effort to supply the army's demands, urged that the available strength should not be wasted in 'bloody and indecisive siege operations.' 'The power of the defensive,' he wrote, when presenting the munitions programme in October 1917, 'has produced a deadlock, and the British Army is destined to be a holding force throughout 1918 until the Americans can become a decisive factor.'

No order to stop or to go slow was, however, sent to G.H.Q. When it was learnt that the removal of Sir Douglas Haig would entail the resignation of the C.I.G.S., with, possibly, disastrous repercussions among the public and the troops, who had full belief in 'Wully,' as he was affectionately called, and implicit trust that the Commander-in-Chief would do his best for them,[2] the attempt to supersede Haig was dropped. But, as will be seen, on the 16th February 1918, Robertson was superseded as C.I.G.S. by Sir Henry Wilson and given another appointment.

Much has been said—without exaggeration as regards the last four weeks—of the dreadful conditions under which the British and Dominion troops fought. No other troops would have stuck to the task asked of them in the same way: determination to defeat the enemy came foremost. It must be remembered that the Ypres Salient, exposed as it was to ground-observed artillery fire from three sides, had a bad name with the troops, and hardly a night passed in the medium artillery zone without heavy shelling and some bombing, and sleep was impossible. Further, that there were no communication trenches, nor tunnels (as at Vimy) to the front, so that reinforcements had to go up and wounded had to be brought down over the open, a trying

---

[1] See Wilson ii, pp. 16–17.

At the time, French was commanding the troops in the United Kingdom having been superseded by Haig in France in December 1915. Wilson was unemployed, having been removed from his last appointment as Chief Liaison Officer with the French as 'persona non grata.'

[2] See, *inter alia*, W. B. Maxwell, in 'Time Gathered,' p. 243: 'We believed firmly in Haig. We trusted him absolutely. We followed him blindly.'

ordeal, all round the clock. Mud did greatly add to the misery and discomfort; it was not the mud, however, but the myriads of shell craters, often
with water in them, which were the effective military obstacle, which prevented the infantry from keeping up to the barrage and the tanks from
manœuvring, which interfered with the supply of ammunition, and which
formed a fatal handicap to the rapid exploitation of successes.

Mud was no novelty in Flanders, as most well-read people know, if not
from the history of Marlborough's campaigns (referred to in the final
chapter) at least in connection with the classic phrase, 'our Armies swore
terribly in Flanders.'

Both the weather and state of the ground are discussed in the course of the
narration. All that need be said here is that mud in war is not unusual, that
conditions on the enemy's side are depicted by him as much worse, and this
is borne out by the fact that the British sick list compared with other years
was 'comparatively slight,' that of the Germans very heavy.

According to the Australians, as will be shown, the mud conditions were
worse in October 1916 on the Somme than at Passchendaele—and no reflec-
tion has ever been cast on the commanders in that battle for continuing
operations into November. General Joffre indeed protested against closing
them down.

Neither the Canadian Corps nor the Australian Corps, both of which
were employed in the last stages of Passchendaele, made complaint of the
conditions at the time or have done so since; they tackled the adverse conditions as part of the war and overcame them, as Sir Douglas Haig expected
they would.

The successes of General Plumer in September and October are almost
unknown to the British public although three times his Army broke through
the much-vaunted German defence systems, causing the enemy to admit his
failure (*Misserfolge*) to himself, and to review and change his defensive tactics
again and again.[1] Yet the Battle of Broodseinde, 'which nobody has ever
heard of,' put the Second Army on the top of the Ypres Ridge, and was
regarded by General Plumer as 'the best thing done by the Second Army,
as we had so little time to prepare'; the Germans speak of it as 'the black day
of the 4th October,' on which 'the German losses, particularly prisoners,
were terrifyingly (*erschreckend*) great.'[2]

With the experience of the previous October on the Somme in his mind,
Sir Douglas Haig might well have brought the battle to a close after
Broodseinde; but, as he wrote to Major-General Sir John Davidson after one
of the periodic attacks on himself,[3]

    'the mere suggestion of *a pause* in our attacks in the north at once
    brought Pétain in his train to see me and beg me to put in another effort

[1] See Note at end of Chapter XV.
[2] Flandern 1917, p. 12 and p. 124.
[3] See *The Times* newspaper of 14th November 1934, when Major-General
Davidson published the letter. The statements in the letter were never questioned
by General Pétain.

against Passchendaele without delay. Knowing as I did what the rotten[1] state of the French Army was in 1917 (for Pétain told me more than once about his awful anxieties), I felt thankful when the winter came and the French Army was still in the field.'[2]

Not a voice was raised against the continuance of the battle, not even in the War Cabinet at this stage, that is after the victory of Broodseinde. Had the French, Belgian and British armies been homogeneous like those of the German kingdoms and principalities, the main operation in Flanders might have been stopped or slowed down, and, say, a dozen divisions sent to the French area to turn the Battle of Malmaison from a limited major raid into a well-exploited victory. But equipment, ammunition and rations being different, such a transfer would have taken long to prepare and could no more have been concealed than the change of garrison on the coast at Nieuport, which only brought disaster.

The Australian Official History—and the Australian Corps was engaged in the final stage—puts this question:

'Let the student, looking at the prospect as it appeared at noon on 4th October, ask himself: "In view of three step-by-step blows [20th, 26th September and 4th October, the battles of Menin Road Ridge, Polygon Wood and Broodseinde] all successful, what will be the result of three more in the next fortnight?" '

Yet, if Haig had brought the operations to an end on the 5th October he would undoubtedly have been blamed for not continuing the struggle, as Ludendorf has been condemned for stopping the great offensive against Hazebrouck and the coast on the 30th April 1918, when the advancing German troops were struggling in the mud and water of the Lys valley, and he feared that a counter-attack might overwhelm them.

The effect of the battles was correctly gauged at the time by the British Intelligence. Its reports 'about broken German divisions, heavy German casualties and diminishing German morale,' and its claim that the enemy had been 'shattered in spirit and in reserves,' were not 'cooked' in order to mislead the War Cabinet. They have since been fully confirmed by Field-Marshal Crown Prince Ruprecht of Bavaria, in chief command opposite the British, by his Chief of the Staff, General von Kuhl, by the German official monograph on the battle, 'Flandern,' and the German Official Account.

In the first case, such was the effect of the Allied onslaught that Crown Prince Ruprecht actually considered and prepared a retirement from the Flanders front. This is what General von Kuhl, his Chief of Staff, has to say on the subject:

[1] Note by Major-General Sir John Davidson. The word 'rotten' was in Haig's letter, but was cut out by the newspaper concerned.

[2] General Pétain, on the 10th October, was still appealing for the protection afforded by the British attacks. Charteris ii, p. 259.

It has been suggested in view of the after-events of his life, that his spirit was broken by his anxieties during the long continuance of the mutinies.

'About the middle of October, the greater part of the divisions on the rest of the front of the Group of Armies [which extended from La Fère (15 miles south of St. Quentin) to the sea] had already been engaged in Flanders. On the whole front outside Flanders, even at the most threatened places like Lens and St. Quentin, we had no more than the very minimum of defenders to meet any diversion attacks which might be attempted. The Supreme Command, which hitherto had helped as far as its reserves permitted, was now, in view of the general situation, hardly in a position to provide reinforcements from the other Groups of Armies on the Western Front. It was, amongst other things, reckoned that the French would proceed to partial attacks to fix German forces on other parts of the front. This actually happened on the 23rd October at Malmaison. Crown Prince Ruprecht found himself compelled to consider whether in the case of his forces proving inadequate, in spite of the many disadvantages involved thereby [including the abandonment of the Flanders coast], he should not withdraw the front in Flanders so far back that the Allies would be forced to carry out an entirely new deployment of their artillery. The time gained thereby could be used for the building of a new defence front, with a shortening of its length and consequent economy of troops. The loss of ground and the moral disadvantage of retirement would have to be accepted. Preparations were duly made for this operation.'

On the 11th October Crown Prince Ruprecht reported to O.H.L. that, 'in order to save material and men, it may become necessary to withdraw the front so far from the enemy that he will be compelled to make a fresh deployment of his artillery.'

Then the October rains came, 'our best ally,' as the Prince entered in his diary on the 12th October. It was a close call, and the German General Staff publication on the lessons of 1914–18 admits that 'Germany had been brought near to certain destruction (*sicheren Untergang*) by the Flanders battle of 1917'—and thereby was compelled to attack in 1918, as the last chance of victory, with inadequate forces, and so lost the War.

What the British offensive had cost the German Armies is summed up in Crown Prince Ruprecht's Order of the Day of the 5th December 1917:

'88 divisions (22 of them twice) the mass of the artillery reserve (*Heeresartillerie*), and other arms and formations of the central reserve have taken part in this, the most prodigious (*gewaltigsten*) of all battles so far fought. Divisions disappeared by dozens into the turmoil of the battle, only to emerge from the witches' cauldron after a short period, thinned and exhausted, often reduced to a miserable remnant, and the gaping spaces left by them were filled by fresh divisions.'

The official explanation of the 'disaster' of the 4th October is that 'the divisions were no longer what they had been, as a result of nervous exhaustion, fatigue and bloody losses.'

Under the 11th October, Crown Prince Ruprecht records in his diary: 'most perturbing is the fact that our troops are steadily deteriorating.'

Accounts from the rank and file tell a dismal story. 'Owing to the constant rain and the exertions of bringing up ammunition, rations and water through the mud, there was much sickness, and nearly everyone had diarrhœa'; as early as July marauding and thieving were rife, and if the field gendarmerie interfered the soldiers 'made short business of the gendarmes.'

Major-General Sir John Headlam, who had seen many battlefields, remarked of the 3rd August battlefield that it was 'the only one in which he had seen a remarkably greater number of German than British casualties.' With this the head of the Intelligence agreed.

Kuhl tells us that even 'The Hell of Verdun' was surpassed, and that in Germany the Flanders battle has been called 'the greatest martyrdom of the World War.' As regards wastage and loss of numbers, he thus depicts the state of the German army after the Flanders battle:

'The supply of reinforcements (*Ersatzlage*) was bound to become even more difficult in the ensuing years, so that in the end the conduct of the War was definitely influenced by it. On this point Field-Marshal Haig has been quite right: if he did not actually break through the German front, the Flanders battle consumed the German strength to such a degree that the harm done could no longer be repaired. The sharp edge of the German sword had become jagged.'

And the morale of the German nation was broken. One of the stoutest of the German corps commanders makes this point:

'In millions of letters from the Western Front from April to November came the ever-rising bitter complaints of the almost unbearable hardships and bloody losses in the scarcely interrupted chain of battles: Arras, Aisne-Champagne [Nivelle], Flanders, Verdun and the Chemin des Dames [Malmaison]. A hundred thousand leave men told the Home Front by word of mouth the details of the ever-growing superiority of the enemy, particularly in weapons of destruction.'

The campaign was fought by Sir Douglas Haig, on a front favourable on account of its strategic advantages, in order to prevent the Germans falling upon the French Armies, shaken and dispirited after three years of unceasing warfare and finally mutinous in consequence of the losses in and failure of the Nivelle offensive, upon which such great hopes had been set. The campaign was sanctioned by the War Cabinet in consequence of the demands of the Admiralty that the Flemish coast must be cleared of the enemy. Incidentally, it was designed to drive the Germans off the high ground from which they had observation over the whole Ypres Salient. In its essential purpose and its incidental purpose, the campaign was certainly successful, but the coastal operation had to be abandoned because it depended on the previous possession of the Ypres Ridge, and the Second Army's success in obtaining possession came too late in the season. Of the efficiency of the main operation there is no doubt. The German Official History tells at length the failure of the High Command to exploit the Nivelle disaster and 'to settle finally with the French Army.' The outstanding reason given is that all available reserves in infantry, guns and ammunition were required to meet the succession of British offensives in Flanders during the summer and autumn of 1917.

In May, and again in June, the German Crown Prince, commanding the Group of Armies which had defeated Nivelle, proposed an attack in strength across the Aisne, opposite Paris, to test the condition of the French defences. 'No one,' says the German Official History, 'could have been more eager to give the order to attack than the High Command, if this had been considered possible; but it was unable to do so.' An estimate was made that such an attack would require 30 divisions, but only 23 were available, of these 'eight were already (in early June) on their way to strengthen the Northern Group of Armies in order to meet the British offensive in Flanders which appeared imminent.' Actually about this time, as Monsieur Painlevé, the French War Minister, has revealed, only two reliable French divisions stood between Soissons (on the Aisne) and Paris.

The campaign had done even more than achieve two of its three purposes: the Germans claim that it affected the campaign of 1918 and the issue of the War; for it had exhausted their reinforcements, so that there was nothing left but the 1899 Class (18-year-olds, just called up) and recovered sick and wounded, whilst in the United Kingdom there were at the end of the year a total of 74,403 officers and 1,486,459 other ranks, more than the total of 1,097,906 of the British Forces in France and Flanders, with 607,400 trained men immediately available—why they were not sent over to France is a matter dealt with in the story of 1918.

The campaign has been called an 'unjustifiable gamble.' War is a gamble. General Sir Charles Harington has written: 'I do not know that any operation of war can be anything but a gamble unless the enemy tells you what he has got on the other side of the hill and the state of his troops.' High authorities, already quoted, regarded this particular gamble in 1917 as justifiable. The war of 1939–45 has exhibited much more desperate gambles, among them Dieppe and Arnhem and our great landings.

The writer has permission to quote from a private letter written to him by Marshal of the Royal Air Force Viscount Trenchard as regards 'Passchendaele.' The passage runs:

'Tactically it was a failure, but strategically it was a success, and a brilliant success—in fact, it saved the world.

'There is not the slightest doubt, in my opinion, that France would have gone out of the War if Haig had not fought Passchendaele, like they did in 1940 in this war, and had France gone out of the War I feel, as all our man-power was in France, we should have been bound to collapse, or, at any rate, it would have lengthened the War for years.'

An anonymous writer in 'Blackwood' has summed up:

'Had the enemy been able to take the offensive against the French, nothing could have saved France from defeat and Britain from a Dunkirk of disastrous proportions. That the Germans were unable to reap their advantage is entirely due to Haig's operations at Passchendaele.'

The opinion of Lieutenant-General Hunter Liggett, commander of the American First Army, on 'Passchendaele' also seems to deserve quotation, as that of a very great soldier who was in France at the time.

'They [the British] paid more for it than they could afford, more than it was worth in itself, but they had no choice. They had to ding-dong away, for Italy was all but out of the fighting and the French were just returning to it.

'The failure of Nivelle's offensive left the British to bear the brunt of the War in the West for most of the year. They battled through Flanders all the summer to such effect that the Germans were unable to exploit the near débâcle of the French.'

Our former enemies are of the same opinion. Their official view is:

'There remained to the Allies as their one positive gain from the Flanders battle the certainty that, by tying down the Germans under intensely severe strain, they survived the crisis which arose in the interval between, on the one side, the breakdown of Russia, the onset of the unlimited submarine campaign, and the reverse of the French in April [Nivelle offensive] and, on the other side, the hoped-for time when American help would begin to be effective. In the year 1918 it turned out that their success definitely contributed to the result that the war ended in favour of the Allies; but when the Flanders battle was broken off they had no inducement to look on it as decisive.[1]

'There can be no doubt to-day . . . that in point of fact English stubbornness bridged over the crisis in France. . . . The help which England brought to the cause of the Entente was justified by the result.'[2]

The German Official History, published in 1942 'For Official Use Only,'[3] thus sums up:

'The offensive had protected the French against fresh German attacks, and thereby procured them time to re-consolidate their badly shattered troops. It compelled O.H.L. to exercise the strongest control over and limit the engagement of forces in other theatres of war; two divisions on their way from the East for Italy [Caporetto] had to be diverted from Italy to Flanders. But, above all, the battle had led to an excessive (*übergross*) expenditure of German forces. The casualties were so great that they could no longer be covered, and the already reduced battle strength of battalions sank significantly lower.'

[1] Flandern 1917, p. 142.
[2] Kuhl ii, p. 110.
[3] Volume xiii, p. 97. See Book List.

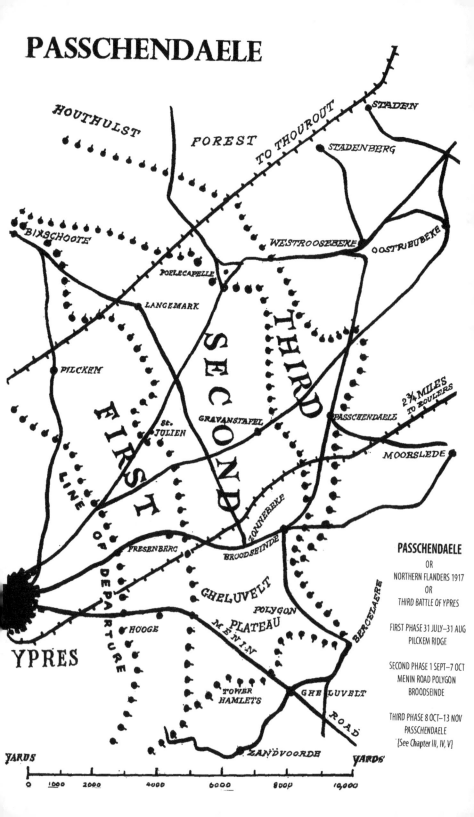

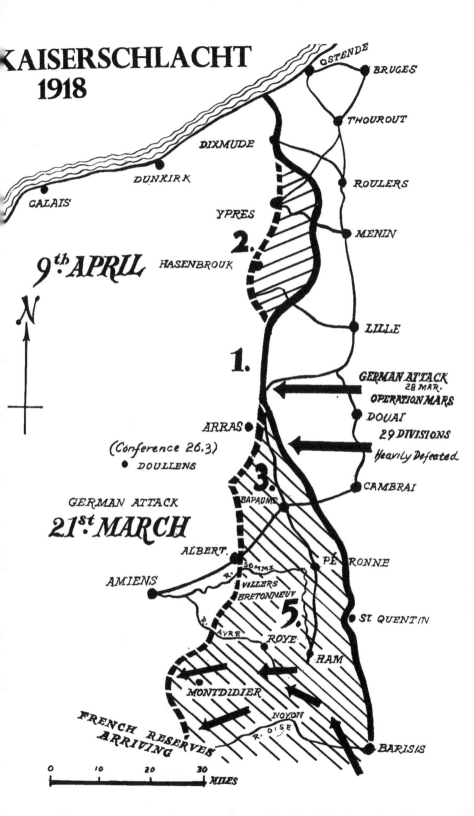

Map scale: 3 inches to 40 miles

OSTEND

NIEUPORT

FRENCH, B
& BR.

DIXMUNDE

2 YPRES

2

MENIN

CALAIS

DUNKIRK

5

LILLE

BRITISH

BETHUNE

GERMAN WITH
RESULT OF

BRITISH BA

N &

1

DOUAI

ARMIES

1

ARRAS

HINDENBURG LINE

DOULLENS

CAM

AUGUST 8

3

3

ALBERT

PÉRONNE

R SOMME

AMIENS

4

4

4

CHAULNES

ST. Q

R AVRE

ROYE

FRE

R OISE

MONTDIDIER

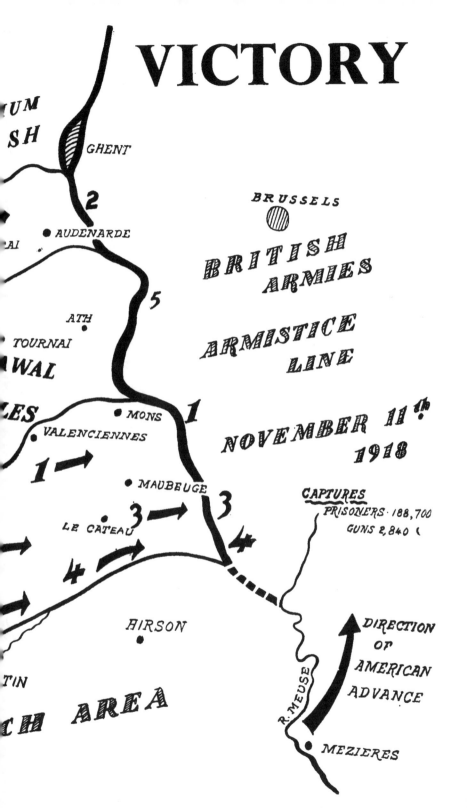